THE SECRET *of* LIFE

The Secret of Life:
Paul's Christ-Centered
Philosophy in Philippians

The Secret of Life
978-1-7910-3636-2
978-1-7910-3637-9 *eBook*

The Secret of Life DVD
978-1-7910-3640-9

Cover description: The cover features a classic painting of the apostle Paul seated among books and manuscripts, deep in thought as he studies and writes by the glow of warm light. The image conveys wisdom, reflection, and spiritual insight, reinforcing the book's exploration of Paul's understanding of the Christian life in Philippians. The cover prominently displays the title, *The Secret of Life*, along with the subtitle, *Paul's Christ-Centered Philosophy in Philippians* in the middle of the cover with the author's name, F. Scott Spencer, at the top of the cover.

Cover Image Credit: Rembrandt Harmenszoon Van Rijn, *Saint Paul in Prison*, 1627, oil on panel, 73 cm x 60cm. Staatsgalerie, Stuttgart, Germany. Public domain.

F. SCOTT SPENCER

THE SECRET *of* LIFE

Paul's Christ-Centered Philosophy in Philippians

ABINGDON PRESS | NASHVILLE

The Secret of Life
Paul's Christ-Centered Philosophy in Philippians

Library of Congress Control Number: 2026939165
978-1-7910-3636-2

Continued on page vi.

To beloved grandson

Thomas ("Tommy") Scott Webber

born while I was writing this book

and

to the gracious congregations of

First Baptist Church, Richmond, Virginia,

and

Bethel Baptist Church, Midlothian, Virginia,

who hosted my early teaching sessions

on Philippians

Continued from page iv.

MANUFACTURED IN THE UNITED STATES OF AMERICA

CONTENTS

WATCH YOUR STUDY ANYTIME, ANYWHERE.

Access your *The Secret of Life* videos and leader resources on any device with your Amplify Media account.

Get Started In Two Steps

1 Scan the QR code or go to My.AmplifyMedia.com /amplify/redeem

2 Create your free account and enter your companion code

Companion Code
FSA06Z8B

Once You're In

- Videos and leader resources saved to your account
- Watch anytime on phone, tablet, or TV
- Come back anytime at My.AmplifyMedia.com

Keep Track of Your Log In Info

Email ________________________________

Password ________________________________

Companion code subject to expiration. Code may be redeemed only by the recipient of this book. Code may not be transferred or sold separately. Internet connection required.

AMPLIFY™ MEDIA

FOREWORD

Paul's Got a Secret

One of the most popular shows in the heyday of black-and-white TV was *I've Got a Secret* (1952–1966). It featured a panel of celebrities tasked with asking contestants a series of yes-or-no questions to uncover a surprising secret about their lives. The contestants might be either well-known figures with a quirky secret or ordinary people with a secret claim to fame. In the former category, iconic British actor Boris Karloff, distinguished for his portrayal of Frankenstein's monster in a series of 1930s horror films, appeared on the show in 1954, as panelists ferreted out his secret fear of mice! In the latter category, the forgettable Pete Best appeared in 1964 with the secret that he'd quit his job two years before as the drummer for The Beatles (the truth is, he was let go and replaced by Ringo Starr).

We love secrets. We love uncovering and sharing them. Of course, beyond the playful stage of a game show, exposing shameful and harmful secrets can cause no end of trouble for secret-holders and whistleblowers. But there are good secrets worth airing, such as keys to unlocking happier, healthier, wiser lives. These are the stock-in-trade of the multimillion-dollar self-help industry. Admittedly, these "secret of life" programs vary wildly in quality from the superficial and sensational to the substantial and scientific. But they all scratch an itch for those of us who struggle to live flourishing, fulfilling lives that matter, which is most of us at some point.

On a musical note, certain songs tap into the same existential vein, such as James Taylor's wonderful number "The Secret O' Life," with the opening thesis line: "The secret of life is enjoying the passage of time."[1] Short and sweet, but worth pondering. I'm sure other songs contain such gems, but I'm partial to J. T.

Toward the end of his brief letter to the Philippians, the apostle Paul claims to have found an important life secret: "I have learned to be content with whatever I have.... In any and all circumstances I have learned the secret of being well-fed and of going hungry, of having plenty and of being in need" (4:11-12). That sounds amazing: contentment "in any and all circumstances," good and bad, full and lean. Contentment is not a strong suit in our obsessively consumerist society, where enough is never enough, or so an avalanche of advertising tells us. We may long for contentment deep down but constantly find ourselves ill at ease—dis-eased—by the lure of more things, shinier objects, better circumstances.

Another verse attributed to Paul states, "Of course, there is great gain in godliness combined with contentment" (1 Timothy 6:6) or, as the KJV and NIV more succinctly read, "But godliness with contentment is great gain." Yes, "of course," peaceful contentment is the greatest gain, the truest treasure of godly living that money can't buy. The consuming quest for more stuff is never satisfied or satisfying. But many of us still have a hard time buying into this philosophy of contentment.

When my home church got new pew Bibles years ago, 1 Timothy 6:6 had a telling misprint, I kid you not, that read, "But godliness with contentment is great pain"—not gain! A perverse typesetter out there, perhaps. Or maybe just an honest one. In our modern materialistic culture, the thought of being content with what we have and don't have pains our insatiable egos. But that pain is a telltale sign of the corrosive nature of our restless spirit of discontentment. Most of us are not masochists. We prefer peace over pain, contentment over conflict.

So, Paul, please tell us your great life secret of contentment in Philippians. We're ready to give you a hearing. But be warned: We're not interested in cheap solutions. Cheap doesn't hold up. You get what you pay for, even in the currency of life philosophies.

Paul's Substantial Secret of Life in Philippians

Rest assured, whether or not you agree with everything Paul says in Philippians, his counsel does not come in a cheap package filled with fluffy pleasantries and platitudes. Three substantial dimensions of Paul's secret of life stand out: It is (1) costly, (2) complex, and (3) Christ-centered. I briefly sketch these dimensions, which will become more evident as we proceed through this study.

First, Paul's secret of life is costly not because he charges a steep fee—Paul freely shares his wisdom (no paywall)—but because he has paid a premium price of hard-lived experience. He speaks and writes what he's come to know deep down in "any and all circumstances," including "plenty" of trials and troubles (4:11-12). Case in point: He writes the letter to the Philippians from a Roman prison, with the possibility of not making it out alive, though he hopes and prays for release (1:17-19). And this is no one-off experience but part of Paul's career of missionary service filled with "far greater labors, far more imprisonments, with countless floggings, and often near death" (2 Corinthians 11:23; cf. 11:24-33). So, when Paul repeatedly speaks about joy, peace, and strength in Philippians (1:2-3, 18, 25; 2:2, 17-18, 29; 4:1, 4-14), he does so in the crucible of serious hardships, not from an armchair or ivory tower perch. Assuming Paul's not a madman (though, tongue-in-cheek, he once referred to himself as such [2 Corinthians 11:23]), his witness of contentment amid confinement and other harsh conditions merits a careful hearing.

Second, Paul's secret of life in Philippians is quite complex. So don't expect his testimony to be simple or easy. This doesn't mean his ideas are hard to comprehend due to an elevated tone, tortured logic, or complicated sentences. Such may be true in some of Paul's other writings, as the author of 2 Peter admits: "Our beloved brother Paul wrote... some things... hard to understand" (3:15-16). But not, by and large, in Philippians, which is arguably Paul's most accessible, congenial, and practical correspondence. Yet this writing is no milk diet for spiritual infants (Paul uses this image in 1 Corinthians 3:1-2). It contains plenty of solid food to chew and grow on, food for thought, food for "hearts and minds" seeking the "peace of God, which surpasses all [naïve] understanding" (Philippians 4:7).

By the same token, while this letter contains several memorable verses that might serve as life mottos, none of them fully captures Paul's philosophy. His secret of life cannot be reduced to pat slogans or "simple steps to successful living." In Philippians, Paul is thinking through, working out, and writing out his progressive understanding of the meaning of life (cf. 1:12, 25; 2:12-13) in a particular time and place. He's writing an urgent missive for the moment, not a manifesto for the ages, though no doubt he would be pleasantly surprised to know we're still studying Philippians and hearing God's voice through it today!

Third, and most significant, Paul's secret of life in Philippians is thoroughly and unabashedly Christ-centered. "For to me, living is Christ" (1:21). "I regard everything as loss... that I may gain Christ" (3:8). "I can do all things through [Christ] who strengthens me" (4:13). Powerful statements, sizzling with conviction. But don't they also sound like slogans, perfect for bumper stickers, church signs, and mission trip T-shirts—nice and catchy but not all that informative? "Christ Is the Top Secret of Life" is about as meaningful as the Christmas card ditty, "Christ Is the Reason for the Season." Sure, but what does that involve exactly? What reason(s)? You need the whole story of Christ to grasp Christ's significance, not a bare statement or catchphrase.

Likewise, living a life centered in Christ entails much more than saying or displaying Jesus's name at every turn. To be sure, in Paul's view, God has exalted the name of Jesus above all other names (2:9-11). But there's nothing magical in the sound and letters of the name itself: "Jesus," a Greek version of the Hebraic "Joshua," was common in Jewish families. Again, it is the full life story of Jesus of Nazareth that reveals his special saving identity, character, and mission as Lord of all and God's anointed Messiah/Christ.

Others might stake a claim to be Lord (Caesar certainly did) or Christ (messianic pretenders abound in crisis periods), and others called Jesus in the New Testament include "a notorious prisoner called Jesus Barabbas" (Matthew 27:16) and "a certain magician, a Jewish false prophet, named Bar-Jesus" (Acts 13:6). But only the faithful Lord Jesus Christ served by Paul merits total trust and devotion. Others may try to manipulate "the name of the Lord Jesus" (Acts 19:13) for their own advantage without knowing in any meaningful sense who this Jesus is (Matthew 7:21-24; Acts 19:11-16). But only those who commit themselves to knowing and following the Lord Jesus Christ in their daily lives can hope to "gain" the flourishing life he embodies and energizes.

So, Paul, what is this grand "secret" Christ-story you've become immersed in that now drives your entire life for the "good" (Philippians 1:6) and the "better" (1:23)? A quick reading of Philippians might leave us disappointed in what appears to be Paul's bare-bones sketch of Christ's experience in a mere seven verses (2:5-11), nothing close to the Gospel narratives' rich portraits. But Philippians 2:5-11 is a whale of a précis in breathtaking poetic form and panoramic scope, highlighting the main life stages of the divine–human Christ from the beginning of time through eternity. What it lacks in details, it makes up for in dramatic effect, and it provides a dynamic model and mindset for Christ-centered living (2:5) that inform and inspire the entire letter, though not in a systematic or formulaic fashion.

Just as Philippians is no step-by-step guide to general successful living, it's also no handy handbook for specifically Christ-centered discipleship. While it contains valuable teachings, even what we might call life lessons, Philippians is less an instruction manual than an invitation call: a call to active, progressive learning with Paul and other disciples about what "living is Christ" (1:21) and living "in Christ" (1:1, 26, 29) entails. Or to use an athletic image that Paul develops in Philippians 3, it's about participating with Christ himself, together with Paul and other "teammates," in running the marathon race of life through choppy terrain and challenging obstacles with joyous persistence and purpose. It's about crawling, walking, stumbling, falling, getting back up again (and again), hopping, skipping, jumping—and running!

Christ himself is the pacesetter and power source for this life-race. But he's not a flashy superhero. In Paul's view, Christ runs with his followers under the banner of the cross, which is no mere logo but a veritable Roman wooden cross, which he carried (with some help) to his crucifixion. At the heart of the Christ-story in Philippians 2:6-11 is the reference to Christ's humiliating human death—"even death on a cross" (2:8). Wondrously, this is not the finish line for Jesus, as God raises him from the dead and exalts him to be Lord of all creation (2:9-11; 3:10). But Christ's resurrection and exaltation do not erase the marks, memories, and miseries of his crucifixion. He is the dying–living–life-giving Lord and Savior. He continues to carry the cross with his followers (see Luke 9:23) along the rugged course of life as part and parcel of his lifesaving, resurrecting mission.

We're back to considering the cost of a flourishing life in Christ—in this case, the ultimate cost of Christ's life on the cross, which he shares with us and we with him. As Paul expresses it in Philippians, "I want to know Christ and the power of his resurrection and *the sharing of his sufferings by becoming like him in his death*" (3:10; emphasis added). Admittedly, this secret of peaceful, powerful life revealed in suffering and death is one aspect of Philippians that does boggle the mind a bit. We're going to need a healthy dose of wisdom that "surpasses all understanding" (4:7) to fully appreciate Paul's paradoxical philosophy of life and death.

Elsewhere, Paul called the saving cross of Christ a "scandal" by conventional standards (1 Corinthians 1:23, CEB). So we might say that Paul's letter to the Philippians unveils a secret and a scandal, which doubles the intrigue. If I titled this study *The Secret Scandal of Life*, I might sell a few more copies, but I wouldn't be completely honest. The term "scandal" usually conjures up sexual transgression. Sorry to disappoint, but you'll find no sex scandal in Philippians (as in 1 Corinthians 5) or sex talk of any kind, and no secret per se as we usually think of one: no special formula, mystery clue, or protected passcode.

Again, Paul freely invites us on an eye-opening adventure of knowing and following Jesus Christ. Paul shares some helpful discoveries he's made along the way, but he doesn't pretend to have all the answers: "Not that I have already obtained this or have already reached the goal" of fullness of life in Christ, "but I press on to lay hold of that for which Christ has laid hold of me" (Philippians 3:12). At the end of the day, "the day of Christ," he hopes he won't have "run in vain or labor[ed] in vain" (2:16).

Even so, from his prison bunk Paul takes us on an extraordinary spiritual trek in Philippians to gain the mind of Christ (2:5; cf. 1 Corinthians 2:16). Reading and studying this short letter won't give you the final answer key to all life's problems, but it will give you much to think about and "work out" toward better living, which Paul calls "salvation" (Philippians 2:12, NRSV). You might treat it like an exciting treasure hunt or secret mission.

A Note on Cover Art and Bible Versions

The cover art for this study is Rembrandt's inimitable depiction of Paul writing letters from a prison cell. I explore this image in the first chapter to illuminate the setting of Philippians.

Unless otherwise noted, I use the NRSVue (New Revised Standard Version Updated Edition) in quoting the text of Philippians. I indicate other versions by standard abbreviations: CEB (Common English

Bible), KJV (King James Version), NASB (New American Standard Bible), NCB (New Catholic Bible), NIV (New International Version), NKJV (New King James Version), NLT (New Living Translation), NRSV (New Revised Standard Version), and RSV (Revised Standard Version). I also occasionally offer my own version, marked by "my translation."

While this study is designed to be engaging and accessible, not highly technical, I do use some Greek (the language Paul wrote in) and Latin terms, always transliterated in English with accompanying definitions. This helps us gain a better feel for Paul's writing style and the Greco-Roman environment.

CHAPTER 1

Prison Letter

Key Passages
Philippians 1:1-26
Philippians 4:21-23
Acts 16:6-40

We don't know what Paul looked like. First-century visual media—inscriptions, paintings, sculptures, coinage—largely showcased imperial rulers. Caesar's face was plastered everywhere. Paul's face, however, was generally effaced, partly because he proclaimed Christ's sovereignty (not Caesar's) but mostly because he wasn't that important in the Roman scheme of things. Nobody but Caesar was. All hail Caesar!

Even among early Christ-followers, Paul was not universally honored and trusted, not least because of his former virulent opposition to the Christ-movement (1 Corinthians 15:9; Galatians 1:13; Philippians 3:6; 1 Timothy 1:12-15). But after his death, Paul's reputation dramatically improved across Christian history, such that many believers today regard him with high esteem, bordering on idolization, outranked only by Jesus. Not that Paul would agree. He saw himself as "the least of the apostles" (1 Corinthians 15:9), the epitome of "weakness" (2 Corinthians 12:8-10), the "chief" of sinners (1 Timothy 1:15, KJV), the humble "[servant] of Christ Jesus" (Philippians 1:1) to whom all glory belongs. But Paul is no longer around to disabuse his adoring fans of their perception of him.

Many Christians, including me for a long time, entertain various images of the magnificent Paul, in turns heroic, stoic, strong, saintly:

the greatest apostle, the premier witness to Christ, the paragon of Christian faithfulness. Yet these ideal portraits don't entirely fit a rare early description of Paul's appearance. The late second-century apocryphal text Acts of Paul reports that Titus, one of Paul's protégés, "saw Paul coming, a man small of stature, with a bald head and crooked legs, in a good state of body, with eyebrows meeting and nose somewhat hooked, full of friendliness; for now he appeared like a man, and now he had the face of an angel." That's quite a picture!

No one knows how accurate it is, but it's fun to consider: on the one hand, a comic sketch of Paul as short, bald-headed, and bowlegged, with a unibrow and skewed nose, and on the other, a cover boy in a "good state of body" and friendly face with an angelic aura. I imagine Paul laughing in heaven over this preposterous depiction, particularly the latter part. He never claimed to be a looker and conceded his rivals' opinion that "his letters are weighty and strong, but his bodily presence is weak and his speech contemptible" (2 Corinthians 10:10; cf. 1 Corinthians 2:1-5).

Saint Paul in Prison

My favorite visual image of Paul comes much later from the master Dutch artist Rembrandt van Rijn. His painting, *Saint Paul in Prison* (1627), is also purely imaginative but registers closer to the real Paul who wrote letters from prison to the Philippians and Philemon and possibly to the Colossians and Timothy. (Some scholars dispute Paul's authorship of Colossians and 2 Timothy.) Though incarceration limits one's movements and public access, it can provide opportunities for deep reflection on the meaning of life and death and continuing correspondence with beloved supporters and the outside world. Notable twentieth-century examples include Dietrich Bonhoeffer's theological and pastoral letters from Berlin's Tegel prison (1943–1945), Martin Luther King's courageous and prophetic "Letter from Birmingham Jail" (1963), and Nelson Mandela's moving and stalwart letters over a lengthy confinement in four South African prisons (1962–1990).

A jail cell served as a creative crucible for Paul to craft his contemplative, emotive letter to the Philippians. Rembrandt's painting spotlights Paul's thoughtfulness and vision, casting a glow around Paul's head, exposing his receding hairline and imposing frontal dome framed by long frizzy hair and a thick beard (he's not bald). His eyes are small but wide open and overarched by separate raised eyebrows (no unibrow) in a pose of intense concentration. Paul is seated on a benchlike cot wrapped in a thick cloak over two undergarments, suggesting the cell's dank environment. His right elbow rests on a sheaf of papers lying atop a large open book; other books and documents clutter the bed at his right side. His right-hand fingers curl around his mouth and under his nose in classic "Thinker" mode. His left hand rests on the open book and holds a stylus between his index and middle fingers as he ponders what to write. This is serious business for Paul.

Rembrandt's scene corresponds with Paul's plea to Timothy: "When you come [to visit me in prison], bring the cloak that I left with Carpus at Troas, also the books, and above all the parchments [to write on]" (2 Timothy 4:13). Bonhoeffer repeatedly noted how books, letters, and other reading materials inspired him during the long, stressful days of imprisonment and informed his return correspondence. Thoughtful ministers need comforting and challenging written resources (not least sacred scriptures) to stimulate their own comforting and challenging communiqués—an increasingly lost art in our slapdash era of "Insta" posting.

A charming feature of Rembrandt's portrait shows Paul's right bare foot poised on his unstrapped sandal, which itself rests atop a slab of rock on a drab wooden floor. The image fits the stereotype of a rumpled scholar rapt in thought, an absent-minded professor devoid of extraneous thoughts—that is, single-minded (Philippians 2:2, 5; 4:2, 7) and totally absorbed in the project at hand.

Two more ominous elements of the painting merit attention—chains and a sword—positioned close to one another, the first fastened to the bedpost, the second leaning against the bed. But these fearsome symbols of Roman penal authority are tempered by their passive functions: The chains dangle loose from post to floor, and the sword is sheathed with no soldier to wield it. Here, Paul is free to think, write, and move around.

Yet this is no minimum security, Club Fed prison. The signs of Paul's unfreedom and insecurity remain palpable, even if momentarily unused. In the case of Philippians, Paul refers to writing this letter "in chains" (1:13, NIV) under "imperial guard" and a possible death sentence (1:17, 19-26). I will examine this scenario more closely later, but for now, we begin to appreciate that the confidence and contentment Paul expresses in Philippians does not reflect some naïve Panglossian positivism ("It's all for the best") but rather a deeply considered conviction amid "any and all circumstances" (4:12).

Letter from a Roman Jail

We know Paul wrote Philippians from a detention center in the Roman Empire, but we don't know precisely where he was being held. The Philippian congregation, which sent a messenger named Epaphroditus to help Paul (2:25-30; 4:18), obviously knew where he was imprisoned, but Paul never mentions the location in his letter.

The Book of Acts reports that Paul was detained in Roman custody twice, each time for two years, long enough for him to compose Philippians and other letters. Neither of these detainments is especially onerous. The first is in Caesarea, the provincial capital of Roman Judea. Though under military guard, Paul is granted "some liberty" and allowed to receive care packages from friends and supporters (Acts 24:22-27). The second is in the imperial capital of Rome. Paul lives under house arrest in rented lodgings, with no attached shackles (or ankle monitor). He's permitted to receive unlimited visitors and freely share the gospel while waiting to appeal his case before Caesar (Acts 28:16, 23, 30-31).

Acts ends Paul's story without reporting the outcome of this or any further trial.

Though we may presume Paul engaged in some correspondence during both of these two-year custodies, Acts doesn't mention it. And neither of these relatively comfortable internments fits the conditions of "imprisonment," "suffering," "struggle," and possible execution Paul references in Philippians (1:13, 17, 20-22, 30). Many scholars still argue that Paul wrote Philippians from Rome but during a later imprisonment (not the one in Acts). According to early church tradition, he wrote from Rome's Mamertine prison, a dreadful dungeon where Paul languished before his beheading by Emperor Nero. This theory is weakened, however, by Paul's optimism in Philippians that he will be freed (not killed) and by Rome's long eight-hundred-mile distance from Philippi over rough terrain. Though not an impossible trek for Epaphroditus to make, it would have been extremely taxing and time-consuming.

A third city has received more attention in recent years: Ephesus, the provincial capital of Roman Asia (western Turkey). Paul reports having fought in Ephesus with "wild animals" (1 Corinthians 15:32) and suffered excruciating "affliction," "so deadly a peril," as if under a "sentence of death" (2 Corinthians 1:8-10). Here, Paul is short on details and long on drama. He fought no literal lions or other ferocious animals (the popular notion of Christians used as beast bait in Roman arenas is overblown) and received no official death verdict in Ephesus that we know of. We're not even sure he served any time in jail there. But Paul did face considerable threats and dangers, such that, sometimes at least, he "despaired of life itself" (1:8). Again, this doesn't square with Paul's buoyant hope in Philippians that he will be released, but it does resonate with his serious life-and-death concerns in Philippians. Paul's hope is grounded in real life and reasoned thought, not in happy-go-lucky, wish-on-a-star naïvete.

To repeat, we simply don't know where Paul was imprisoned when he wrote Philippians. He experienced numerous punishments and detentions over his apostolic career in various places, including but not restricted to Caesarea, Rome, and Ephesus (see 2 Corinthians 11:23-33). The Paul of Acts bids farewell to the Ephesian church elders with the cheery note that "in every city . . . imprisonments and persecutions are waiting for me" (Acts 20:17-23). Conceding that "every city" exaggerates the point, that still leaves a lot of places where Paul might have written Philippians. The most we can say is that the challenging prison setting behind this letter is typical for Paul. He doesn't write as a privileged elitist milking the odd arrest to burnish a tough-guy reputation. Paul was no *faux* prisoner. He spent many days and nights in multiple holding places suffering for the righteous cause of Christ.

So why, then, spend any time exploring specific writing sites for Philippians? Because it's important to emphasize that Paul did not post weekly newsletter updates of his ordeals to generate "likes" or "cares." Prison tales can be very titillating, even voyeuristic, offering rare glimpses for common folk into jail life (think *Shawshank Redemption*). But Paul didn't write to entertain the public or boost his "brand." Considering possible prison locales reminds us that Paul wrote Philippians from some particular place to a particular people for particular purposes. Further, Paul writes as a particular person (not an avatar or username) with his own peculiar thoughts, feelings, and experiences. This is personal for Paul.

In short, Philippians, like all of Paul's letters, is an occasional writing, responding to distinct situations in Paul's and his audience's lives. Few concepts are more critical to understanding Paul's correspondence. He did not sit at a library table, an office desk, or a retreat center—or on a prison cot—to write a formal philosophy of life, a theology of the Christian faith, or a manual of church order. However inspired he might have felt, he had no intention of composing new Scripture. His Bible, like that of Jesus and his earliest followers, was the Jewish Scriptures, what Christians call the Old Testament. Though today we read Philippians with great profit as part of the New Testament, we should underscore that Paul did not write this letter for us. When we read Philippians, we eavesdrop on others' mail. We do so gratefully and humbly, with due appreciation for the contexts and conditions that birthed this marvelous writing.

Letter to the Philippian Congregation

Compared to our limited knowledge of Paul's writing location, we know considerably more about this letter's destination and target audience. The opening greeting is clear and to the point: "Paul and Timothy, servants of Christ Jesus, To all the saints in Christ Jesus who are in Philippi, with the bishops and deacons" (1:1). Pre-email, we used to write letters on paper using proper form learned in school. We signed our names at the end. Ancient letters, however, typically led with authors' names and descriptions (more like modern memos). Paul often includes companions like Timothy in his greeting, not as full cowriters but as consultants, sounding boards, editors, and secretaries.

Though Timothy was with Paul as he composed this letter, there's no indication he was incarcerated with Paul, who repeatedly refers to "my imprisonment" (1:7, 13, 17). Timothy, one of Paul's dearest associates, is also identified with Paul in introductions to 2 Corinthians, Colossians, 1 and 2 Thessalonians, and Philemon. Paul will have more to say about Timothy later in Philippians, including his plan to send Timothy to Philippi in Paul's stead soon (2:19-24).

Paul writes to one large Philippian group and two subgroups: "all the saints in Christ Jesus . . . with the bishops and deacons" (1:1). These terms sound very pious, official, ecclesiastical—in a word, churchy. Despite referring to "all saints," this language also feels exclusive, intimidating, hierarchical—in a word, clubby. I'm an ordained minister and former seminary professor, but I'm no saint, not even close, and I've never been a bishop or deacon in any church system. So much for Philippians speaking to me or anyone else not named Francis of Assisi or Mother Teresa.

But without engaging in too much linguistic fiddling, we should note that all three terms have more common meanings: "saints" (*hagioi*) can simply represent all ordinary people of God, graciously "made right/holy" to variously serve God and others in their daily lives; "bishops" (*episkopoi*) can refer to "overseers" or "leaders" generally, not limited to high-level clerics; likewise, "deacons" (*diakonoi*) may designate humble "servants" or "ministers" (ordained or not) whom Jesus held up as the "greatest" models for himself and his followers (Luke 22:26; cf. Mark 9:33-37; 10:42-45; Luke 22:24-27).

Paul was a church planter, pastor, and teacher, but not so much an administrator of corporate structures and procedures. He viewed the church less as a business organization than as a living organism: the Spirit-led partnership among all members of Christ's communal body (see 1 Corinthians 12:12-13; Philippians 1:5-7). One reason many scholars dispute Paul's primary authorship of the Pastoral Letters (1 and 2 Timothy; Titus) is that they present a more developed church hierarchy than Paul's other writings, including special rules for bishops, deacons, widows, and elders (1 Timothy 3:1-13; 5:1-22), which Philippians entirely lacks.

Paul addresses the whole Philippian congregation of "saints" in Christ, expecting his letter to be read aloud and discussed, as was the custom, before the entire assembly. A few handwritten copies (manuscripts) might have been made, but far from enough to distribute to every individual or household.

With no available church rolls, it's hard to determine the size of the young Philippian church, but it must have been fairly small, a peculiar, vulnerable minority in Philippi, a cosmopolitan city of 10,000 to 15,000 people in northeastern Greece, near the Aegean Sea. Famous leaders and events associated with Philippi set the political and cultural stage for Paul's eventual introduction of the gospel of Christ. The town was first named "Springs" (*Krenides*) by a group of Greeks called Thasians (from the nearby island of Thasos), who worked the gold mines in the surrounding hills. So we might call the place "Gold Springs" until it was conquered by Philip II of Macedon (356 BCE), refortified, and redesignated as Philippi in the Greek province of Macedonia. Apart from establishing this namesake city, Philip's main legacy was siring Alexander the Great, whose kingdom extended from Greece to India.

Fast-forward two centuries, when the Romans took over Macedonia, and a century beyond that to the momentous transition from Roman Republic to Empire. Not long after Julius Caesar was assassinated by a squad of rebel senators (44 BCE), two of these politicians, Brutus and Cassius, battled with Mark Antony and Octavian for control of the realm. In a showdown on a plain near Philippi, the latter pair proved victorious (42 BCE). Antony first governed Philippi, but that all changed a decade later, when Octavian routed Antony in a decisive naval fight (31 BCE). Consequently, Octavian assumed autocratic rule of the empire, changed his name to Augustus ("Your Majesty"), and adjusted Philippi's full title to *Colonia Iulia Augusta Philippensis* ("Colony of Julius Augustus Philippi"), thus giving the city extensive rights to Roman citizenship, religious ceremony, economic opportunity, and military protection.

The religious environment was enhanced by an array of temples and monuments to Greco-Roman gods, whose ranks now included the emperor himself. Commercial exchange thrived due to Philippi's prime midpoint location on the Egnatian Way, an east–west thoroughfare (interstate highway) running overland 750 miles between the Adriatic and Black Seas. A strong military presence ensured transportation security, and Philippi became a popular settlement place for retired soldiers. I grew up in San Antonio, Texas, a large city with several Army and Air Force bases and a large veteran population. Every church I attended growing up seemed to have a group of vets from World War I through the Korean War and young soldiers dispatched to Vietnam. Memories and experiences of war have profound, lingering effects on community life, even among those who did not participate directly.

Beginnings of the Philippian Congregation

The cosmopolitan character of Philippi is displayed in Acts' narrative of Paul's maiden mission to the city (16:6-40). Scholars differ widely in their opinions of Acts' historical reliability, ranging from pure fiction to proven fact. A middle, moderate position seems wisest to me. Written a couple of decades (or more) after Paul's death, Acts represents an interpretive reflection on the people and events it covers. But that's true of all good history writing, unless you prefer to read a bare-bones chronicle rather than a compelling, well-crafted account.

The author of Acts, the same person who wrote the Gospel of Luke (maybe Paul's associate Luke, though he's not named in either volume), used carefully investigated source material to write a history of Jesus and his early followers (Luke 1:1-4; Acts 1:1-2). But he spun this material from an unabashed pro-Christ perspective. I read Luke and Acts as historical narratives of faith, interpreting the theological significance of past events but not inventing events out of whole cloth, which would provide a shaky basis for faith. I think it's reasonable, then, to take Acts 16 as a generally dependable account of the Philippian fellowship's origins, allowing for various embellishments for dramatic effect.

Let's look at some highlights of Paul's first adventures in Philippi.

Surprise Call from Macedonia (Acts 16:6-12)

Paul tried to plan his missionary itinerary under the Holy Spirit's guidance. But he sometimes drifted from God's positional system (GPS) and had to be brought back on track. At the outset of a new mission journey, Paul and his team, including Silas and Timothy, traveled through Galatia (central Turkey), since the Spirit had steered them away from Asia (western Turkey). But when they determined to head northwest into Bithynia, "the Spirit of Jesus did not allow them" (16:7).

What to do in the face of this roadblock? Since Paul's sense of Spirit-direction seems off, he receives a God-generated night vision of "a man of Macedonia pleading with him and saying, 'Come over to Macedonia and help us'" (16:9). Consequently, Paul and crew sail to the port of Neapolis, from where they travel ten miles on the Egnatian Way to Philippi, "a leading city of the district of Macedonia and a Roman colony" (16:12).

Down by the Riverside (Acts 16:13-15, 40)

In Acts, when Paul comes to a city, he typically first preaches about Christ in the local synagogue to fellow Jews and gentiles sympathetic to Jewish monotheism and ethics. Such gentiles are commonly designated "God-worshippers" or "God-fearers." But Philippi only has a small Jewish community at this time, perhaps not large enough to have a synagogue in town. At any rate, Paul first goes on the Sabbath day outside the city gate to a riverside place, where he speaks to a women's prayer group. This location perhaps suggests a marginal status for the Jewish women and their gentile friends who gather there. Among the latter group, a "God-worshipping" woman called Lydia proves especially receptive to Paul's message. She commits herself to Christ by being baptized, leading her household to follow suit, and welcoming Paul, his companions, and other new Christ-believers into her home.

Lydia is an impressive figure in many ways. She had migrated from Thyatira (in the province of Asia) and reestablished her profitable purple cloth business in Philippi. Evidently, she became successful enough to head her own household (no husband, father, or male relative is mentioned) and own a residence large enough to accommodate servants and guests. She's distinguished in Acts as the first convert to Christ in Roman Greece and the first host/leader of the Philippian "house church." In religious circles today that accept women ministers, she'd be called Pastor or Mother Lydia.

Given her prominence in the community, it's curious that she receives no mention in Paul's Philippian letter. But ten years or so separate Paul's founding mission and his writing of Philippians. By then, Lydia may have moved her trade to a larger market for high-end purple goods. Still, Paul acknowledges two other women leaders, Euodia and Syntyche (Philippians 4:2-3), whom we will consider in chapter 6 of this study.

Fortune-Telling Slave-Girl (Acts 16:16-18)

We don't know the duration of Paul's inaugural stay in Philippi, but it was long enough to attend the outdoor prayer meeting on multiple Sabbaths. On one riverside trip, he's waylaid by a young enslaved female fortune teller who brought her Roman owners considerable income. The slave-girl's psychic oracles supposedly derived from a serpent-agent of the god Apollo who controlled her voice. In other words, she was possessed by an alien spirit-force that her masters manipulated for money.

When she encounters Paul and associates on the street, we naturally expect her to solicit them. But she does nothing of the sort. Instead, she tags along and keeps bellowing, as if on a replay loop, "These men are slaves of the Most High God, who proclaim to you the way of salvation" (Acts 16:17). In a way, she's giving them free publicity. When Paul later writes the Philippian letter, he introduces himself and Timothy as "slaves of Christ Jesus" (Philippians 1:1, CEB) and discusses "salvation" (1:19, 28; 2:12).

But in the Acts scenario, Paul becomes irked at the slave-girl's routine. She may technically be saying the right things, but she seems more like an annoying nuisance than an effective witness. When Paul can't take it anymore, he suddenly turns around and casts out her serpent-spirit. We're not told what happens to her after that. By throttling her prophetic Apollonian powers, Paul renders her useless to her bosses; she remains a vulnerable young female slave, only now with a damaged reputation. We can only hope Lydia and the fledgling

Philippian congregation take her in as a partner "saint in Christ Jesus" (Philippians 4:21).

Paul's First Prison Ordeal (Acts 16:19-24)

As the slave-girl exits the scene, her owners take center stage. Livid over the loss of their money-making slave, they seize Paul and Silas and haul them before Philippi's chief judges. Instead of filing an economic grievance, however, the slave masters up the ante, playing on anti-Jewish, pro-Roman, and law-and-order sentiments: "These men, these Jews, are disturbing our city and are advocating customs that are not lawful for us, being Romans, to adopt or observe" (16:20-21). These emotive, incendiary charges are totally trumped up, except for the fact that Paul and Silas are Jews who believe in Jesus Messiah.

But this was no crime. Overall, the Romans were tolerant of different religious movements, provided they didn't disturb civic peace, disrupt the rule of law, or denounce Caesar outright. Paul and company have been quietly minding their business, sharing the gospel with a small women's prayer group outside of town and Lydia's household in Philippi. Yes, Paul lashes out against a fortune teller (because she keeps disturbing *his* peace), but he's no wild-eyed revolutionary, aiming to colonize Philippi for Christ.

But the slave-girl's owners couldn't care less about legal fine points. They're mad about their financial loss and want their pounds of Paul's and Silas's flesh. And they do succeed in whipping up the crowds in the marketplace and securing the magistrates' punitive verdict against the two preachers, including orders that they be stripped down, severely beaten, thrown into an "innermost cell" (16:24; sounds dungeon-like), shackled by their feet, and placed under tight guard. In a letter written to another Macedonian city, Paul describes this ordeal as being "shamefully mistreated at Philippi" and suffering "great opposition" (1 Thessalonians 2:2). This is missionary Paul's first imprisonment recorded in Acts, an ironic twist on his former work of binding and detaining followers of the Christ-Way (Acts 8:3; 9:1-2).

The crisis in Acts 16 forms an informative backdrop to Paul's Philippian letter but with key distinctions. He's imprisoned in Philippi when he first preaches there. Several years later, he writes to the Philippian congregation from a Roman prison in another city. Further, while Paul has been incarcerated for some (unspecified) time when he writes Philippians, his confinement in the Philippian jail doesn't last one night!

Shaking and Shaming (Acts 16:25-40)

Personally unshaken by their confinement, Paul and Silas pass the time by "praying and singing hymns to God" (16:25) loud enough for the other prisoners to hear. Then suddenly, around midnight, the whole prison is shaken by a violent quake that rips open the prison doors and snaps off the prisoners' chains. Not a welcome event for the main guard, who's prepared to kill himself with his own sword rather than face the consequences of a massive prison break. But amazingly, no one dashes out. Paul and Silas calm the distressed jailer and offer him and his family salvation in "the Lord Jesus" (16:31). The jailer takes the two men home, tends to their wounds, feeds them, and leads his entire household to be baptized, just as Lydia did. Again, there's no mention of this crew in Philippians, but it's nice to imagine that some, even the Roman jailer himself, participated in the Philippian community Paul addresses.

After the seismic jailbreak, the city officials want nothing more to do with this troublesome missionary party. So they now order that Paul and Silas be formally released and quietly sent on their way. But Paul doesn't let the officials "discharge [them] in secret" (16:37). He demands a public apology for the shameful mistreatment of Roman citizens. Uh- oh. That's an important piece of new information in the story. Paul is not only an ethnic-religious Jew; he's also a Roman citizen, from birth no less (see 22:27-29). Roman citizens, not least in a Roman colony like Philippi, were entitled to legal rights of due process and protections from harsh beatings and carceral conditions. No one had bothered to check on Paul's citizenship status. He gets his apology from the officials, even as they implore him to leave town—which Paul does—but not before going to Lydia's house again and receiving encouragement from the believers gathered there (16:40).

It's curious that Paul never refers to his Roman citizenship in his letters. But in Philippians, he twice uses citizenship language to refer to the status of believers in the commonwealth of Christ (Philippians 1:27; 3:20). I will unpack these provocative "citizen" passages in chapter 3.

This survey of the Philippian church's origin story in Acts 16 offers suggestive hints about the congregation's social makeup, worth bearing in mind as we work through the Philippian letter. The Acts narrative features a richly diverse set of characters, including women and men, Jews, God-fearing gentiles, Roman citizens (Paul and Silas), prosperous businesspeople (Lydia), exploited slaves (fortune teller), Roman guards (jailer), and household servants. This mosaic resonates nicely with Paul's statement of Christ-based unity in Galatians 3:26-28, cutting across conventional ethnic, social, and gender boundaries:

> *In Christ Jesus you are all children of God through faith. As many of you as were baptized into Christ have clothed yourselves with Christ. There is no longer Jew or Greek; there is no longer slave or free; there is no longer male and female, for all of you are one in Christ Jesus.*

We will keep an eye on how Paul's unity principle tracks among Jew/gentile, slave/free, and male/female identities in Philippians. We will also pay attention to economic factors dividing rich/poor people, recalling figures in Acts 16, such as the prosperous purple-cloth seller Lydia and the exploited fortune-telling slave-girl. I suggested that Lydia's nonmention in Philippians may indicate she had moved her business elsewhere before Paul wrote this letter. It also raises the prospect that the congregation became poorer through the years with fewer well-heeled, elite-citizen members. We shall see.

Prisoner's Progress

In Philippians, the imprisoned Paul never specifies his accusers or spells out the charges leveled against him. And we should not assume he faced the same criminal charges of disturbing Roman peace and defying Roman law (reported in Acts 16:20-21) in every city he visits as if he's on Interpol's "Most Wanted" list. We might also presume the Philippians already know the present case against Paul (such news traveled fast); if so, they need interpretation more than information. *So we hear you're in jail, Paul—again! What purpose does this confinement serve? What does this do for your reputation—and ours?*

Paul is big on divine purpose or "providence," as it's traditionally called. He's convinced God operates in and through him "in any and all circumstances," pleasant and painful, to bring about God's good purposes (Philippians 1:6, 19; 2:13; 4:12). This is not a naïve optimism ("the power of positive thinking," "put on a happy face") but rather a gritty partnership with God and other believers working out God's saving aims together (2:12) amid life's multifaceted experiences. Paul characterizes his belief in providence in terms of "progress" (1:12, 25)—again, not some blithe sense of "every day in every way it keeps getting better" but a deep-seated conviction that things are moving in the right direction, God's direction.

Okay, Paul, if you say so. But seriously, what's so progressive about prison, apart from the prospect of getting out! Well, Paul does hope to get out and "continue with all of you for your progress and joy in faith" (1:25). But he also dares to claim progress during his detainment:

> *I want you to know, brothers and sisters, that what has happened to me has actually resulted in the progress of the gospel, so that it has become known throughout the whole imperial guard and to everyone else that my imprisonment is for Christ, and most of the brothers and sisters, having been made confident in the Lord by my imprisonment, dare to speak the word with greater boldness and without fear.*
>
> *(Philippians 1:12-14)*

That's an incredible statement, setting an encouraging, "confident" tone for the whole letter. Notice the focus on three parties: (1) Christ, (2) the imperial guard, and (3) brothers and sisters in Christ.

"For Christ"

Paul makes a stunning connection between his confinement and Christ. Somehow, his "imprisonment is for Christ" (1:13). How can that be? It's hard to see how Paul's shackling in a jail cell could be for Christ's sake or benefit. What would Christ gain from this misfortune? Why would Christ want his apostle to suffer?

Perhaps, to take another tack, Paul discloses the main reason he's in custody: namely, for/because of preaching Christ. The historian Suetonius commented that Emperor Claudius expelled all Jews from Rome in 41 CE because of repeated turmoil over a figure called "Chrestus," which may be a misspelling of "Christus/Christ." The details of the disturbance remain fuzzy. Remember, in any case, that honoring a non-Roman religious hero—like "Christ," the Jewish Messiah—was not automatically illegal, unless accompanied by overt condemnations of Caesar and/or actionable militant plots against the government.

This was simply not Paul's m.o. Subtle swipes against Caesar and his kingdom, yes. Key words like "peace," "Lord," and "gospel"—which Paul identifies with Jesus Christ in the opening verses of Philippians (1:3, 7, 12)—all have Roman counterparts: Roman "peace" (*pax*) through conquest, Caesar as sovereign "Lord" of the realm, and "good news" (gospel) of Roman battle victories. Paul is all about Christ, not Caesar. "For to me, living is Christ" (1:21). Paul is more pro-Christ than anti-Caesar, so consumed by Christ, so in love with Christ that it's fair to say he has little energy left for antagonistic pursuits and bitter grievances.

This leads me to favor another translation: "my chains are in Christ" (1:13, NKJV). The subject change from "imprisonment" to "chains" is not significant, since the Greek term can refer to both the physical instrument (chains) and a general state of imprisonment. The Greek preposition, however, admits a wider range of meanings, including "in," "on," "at," "by," "with," and "for"—with "in" best fitting most contexts and "for" the fewest. Throughout his writings, Paul most often characterizes believers' relationship with Christ as participating "in Christ" (see 1:26, 29; 2:5; 3:3, 9, 14; 4:7, 19, 21). "In-Christ-one" closely approximates "Christian," a label used only three times in the New Testament (Acts 11:26; 26:28; 1 Peter 4:16), never by Paul.

I suggest, then, that Paul fundamentally frames his imprisonment "in Christ" to express his deep sense of being infilled with and enfolded by Christ—especially by Christ's love, hope, peace, and joy—all core emotive attitudes in Philippians. Paul feels and knows this dynamic Christ-connection in his bones, and he wants all fellow Christ-devotees and everyone he contacts—including the imperial guard—to feel, know, and live in this same Christ energy field.

"Throughout the Whole Imperial Guard"

It's surprising to hear Paul's shout-out to the Roman imperial guard (*praetorian*)—the only mention of this military police force in his letters—in a neutral, and possibly positive, tone. Actually, Paul seems to reference this same group by another name at the end of Philippians in unmistakably congenial terms: "Greet every saint in Christ Jesus. The brothers and sisters who are with me greet you. All the saints greet you, especially those of the emperor's [Caesar's] household" (Philippians 4:21-22). Here, "household" should be taken as a broad marker of Caesar's subjects and servants, not members of his immediate family. Caesar rather fancied himself as the Great Father (*Paterfamilias*) of everyone in the empire.

Imperial police stations and administrative centers were established in cities across the realm. Apparently, some imperial guardsmen not only became aware of Paul's "imprisonment in Christ" but were also impressed enough by his Christ-focused witness and demeanor (how he coped in confinement) to believe in Christ themselves and, on some level, associate with the local group of "in-Christ-ones." A remarkable turn of events, wonderfully reminiscent of the Philippian jailer's embracing Christ and his missionaries in Acts 16:30-34.

"Most of the Brothers and Sisters"

The guards of the special corps were not the only ones affected by Paul's confinement "in Christ." Indeed, Paul claims his imprisonment has boosted confidence "in the Lord" for most Christ-advocates to proclaim the gospel themselves "without fear" (Philippians 1:14). As prisoner Paul persists in boldly advancing the cause of Christ and joyously participating in the life of Christ, he inspires believers with more freedom to move about, speak their minds, and join their voices with Paul in a swelling gospel chorus.

Yet Paul admits that mixed motives drive these new Christ-campaigners. On the one hand, some sincerely "proclaim Christ out of love," "from goodwill"—toward both Christ and Paul—supporting Paul's mission and even serving as witnesses for his "defense" (1:15-16). On the other hand, unfortunately, some operate "from envy and rivalry" and "out of selfish ambition," seizing the opportunity of Paul's detention and potentially damaged reputation to bolster their own statuses at Paul's expense (1:15-17). While the lion apostle is away, his mousy rivals can play.

Sadly, then as now, the church is not exempt from petty power struggles, as illustrated, for example, in 1 Corinthians 1–3, 2 Corinthians 10–13, and Galatians 1–2. Sometimes Paul takes the bait, aggressively defending his integrity and attacking his opponents. He does a little of that in Philippians (3:2-6, 17-21), but not much. Overall, in this letter, Paul strikes a more conciliatory tone, not least in his remarkably chill reaction to his competitors' preaching. "What does it matter?" Paul muses. "Just this, that Christ is proclaimed in every way, whether out of false motives or true, and in that I rejoice" (1:18). What an enviable attitude! Paul chooses joy over jockeying for power, the bright side over the bitter shadow, what truly matters—promoting Jesus Christ—over what could elevate his own ministerial career.

CHAPTER 2

Thank-You Letter

Key Passages
Philippians 1:3-11
Philippians 4:10-20

Good manners are not entirely dead in our ever-more-uncivil society. Many parents and schoolteachers still urge children to say "Please" and "Thank you," and most kids are happy to comply, at least when they're young.

On the verge of going extinct, however, are old-fashioned handwritten thank-you notes. If there's an upside to this trend, I feel more appreciated when someone still takes the time to pen a personal message rather than shoot off an email. Psychological science affirms the value of gratitude over grievance for individual and social well-being. Giving thanks is good for body, soul, and society—especially in difficult circumstances. Not some mind trick about the benefits of pain, but a mindful perception of pleasant memories and present joyful experiences amid suffering. It's this gratitude to God, Christ, and the Philippian congregation that sustains Paul in his imprisonment, that comprises one secret ingredient of his contentment in confinement.

It's notable that within the thin outer frame of the first and final greetings (Philippians 1:1-2; 4:21-23) Paul constructs a thicker inner frame of thanksgiving around the Philippian correspondence (1:3-11; 4:10-20), giving it the character of a thank-you letter—which is not to trivialize or sentimentalize it. Paul's gratitude is deeply considered, not slapdash; intensely emotional, but not sappy.

In the final main section, Paul does not say thanks per se. But his opening "I rejoice" (*echarēn*) in 4:10 closely associates with the opening "I thank" (*eucharistō*) in 1:3. Emotional attitudes of gladness and gratitude intertwine. Also, Paul's comment in Philippians 4:14-15—"It was kind of you [all] to share [together] my distress.... No church shared with me [like you did] in the matter of giving and receiving"—reflects a thankful heart for the Philippians' support. It also reveals the experience of sharing life's hardships as a cornerstone for gratitude.

In everyday English, "share" connotes a nice thing to do, especially for polite children again ("share your toys"), but not so necessary and perhaps detrimental for grown-ups aiming to get their *fair share* (think lucrative stock *shares*) in a competitive market. While "share" is a suitable translation, the Greek term *koinōnia* carries richer meanings beyond kindergarten playrooms and corporate boardrooms. *Koinōnia* is familiar to many Christians, typically associated with "fellowship," another correct but somewhat squishy rendering evoking social get-togethers in church *fellowship* halls. Nothing wrong with church folk eating and playing together (much better than bickering and backbiting). But this notion only scratches the surface of the *koinōnia* that inspires Paul's gratitude.

The *koinos* root, meaning "common," evokes notions of commonality, community, communion, a deep and wide sharing of interlaced common life in Christ, as Paul believes. And not just statically or status-wise, but actively and equally. In other words, *koinōnia* involves dynamic partnership and participation. The NRSVue hits this right note in Paul's opening thanksgiving: "I thank my God for every remembrance of you [all]... for your partnership [*koinōnia*] in the gospel from the first day until now" (1:3, 5). "I hold you in my heart, for all of you are my [joint] partners [*sygkoinōnous*] in God's grace" (1:7; cf. 2:1).

Beyond the "heart"-felt emotional dimensions of Paul's grateful partnership with the Philippians, we should also bear in mind economic and political elements underlying this thank-you letter.

On the economic side, *koinōnia* applied to business partnerships or associations, ideally for the mutual benefit of all parties. In the early Christ-communities, the goal was not accumulating as many "shares" of the "company" as possible for one's portfolio but rather sharing together monies, goods, and services for the common good, the commonwealth.

Acts describes the radical financial ethos of the first Jerusalem church: "All who believed were together and had all things in common [*koina*]; they would sell their possessions and goods and distribute the proceeds to all, as any had need" (Acts 2:44-45; cf. 4:32-35). As far as we know, the Philippian congregation did not adopt this "sell all" practice. But their relationship with Paul revolved in no small measure around material issues: "No church shared [*ekoinōnēsen*] with me in the matter of giving and receiving except you alone" (Philippians 4:15). Let's take a look at the terms and conditions of these exchanges, for which Paul is grateful.

Where money is involved, politics inevitably follows. And strange as it sounds, so too with thanks, teetering on the fault line between pure gift (no strings attached) and incurred debt (you owe me one). The common phrase "debt of gratitude" betrays a power inequity between giver and receiver, benefactor and beneficiary. Political strongmen fancy themselves as benevolent overlords of the masses who owe them gratitude—and servitude. These narcissistic dictators get very offended if their subjects fail to shower them with thanks, which they would never stoop to return. "Thanks for your service," if uttered at all, is a throwaway line. All thanks are due the sovereign ruler.

Some scholars argue that Paul skates close to the self-sufficient, authoritarian edge in the Philippian letter, particularly at the end. According to this interpretation, at best, Paul is a reluctant, begrudging thanksgiver. "Not that I am referring to being in need" (4:11). Read: "I don't really need your help, certainly not as much as you need mine. The 'gifts' you've sent are nice but no more than what you owe me.

Let's not forget who's the great apostle here." I think this cynical take misreads Paul's intentions. But there are complications to tease out, as always when emotions, economics, and politics intersect.

Thankful for the Philippians' Partnership in Gospel Ministry

After offering common greetings such as "Grace" and "Peace" associated with religious blessings, ancient letter authors customarily offered thanksgivings and well-wishes for the addressees' good fortune and health. This set a congenial mood, making subsequent critical comments easier to swallow. As elsewhere in Paul's letters (except for Galatians, where he's so upset he plunges right into attack mode), in Philippians, Paul extends the spirit of grace and peace with kind expressions of thanks and prayers (1:3-11). This section is similar to 1 Thessalonians 1:2-10, addressed to another church in Macedonia, located about one hundred miles southwest of Philippi on the Egnatian Way.

Paul, however, does not simply follow standard letter-writing conventions but adapts them to forward his God- and Christ-centered gospel. Grace, peace, thanks, and prayers flow "from God our Father and the Lord Jesus Christ" (1:2). The spiritual partnership with the Philippians that fires Paul's gratitude is forged "in God's grace," suffused "with the tender affection of Christ Jesus," and produces a bountiful "harvest of righteousness that comes through Jesus Christ for the glory and praise of God" (1:7-8, 11).

And Paul does not say these things as mere formalities to be forgotten when he gets down to the heart of his message. They are the beating heart of this letter, striking the dominant chord for everything that follows, succinctly echoed in the last chapter: "Do not be anxious about anything, but in everything by prayer and supplication with thanksgiving let your requests be made known to God. And the peace of God, which surpasses all understanding, will guard your hearts and your minds in Christ Jesus" (4:6-7). (I will unpack this key text in chapter 6.)

The deeply emotional tone of Paul's thankful introduction merits close attention in relation to three aspects commonly discussed by emotion analysts: (1) duration, (2) intensity, and (3) intelligence.

Duration: Long-Lasting

Emotions can range from knee-jerk impulses, like a jolt of fear upon seeing a serpentine brown object in the grass before registering it's just a crooked stick, to persisting mood states, like deep-seated depression or anxiety. This applies to positive emotions, too, like a quick spark of awe from glimpsing a soaring hawk or an abiding sense of joy from a lifelong friendship.

This last example fits to a tee Paul's relationship with his Philippian friends in Christ. Their joyous bond, their "partnership in the gospel" for which Paul gives sincere thanks, unfolds from "the first day until now" (1:5) "until the day of Jesus Christ" (1:6, 10) in three stages:

- *Past*: the first day of Paul's mission in Philippi, including a brief imprisonment (Acts 16:23-27)
- *Present*: now, some years later, when Paul writes to the Philippians from prison
- *Future*: the day of Jesus Christ, a common shorthand for the time of Christ's climactic return to earth

Christians today often refer to this final event as "the second coming," though that wording never appears in the Bible. The New Testament favors the language of "appearance" (*parousia*), along with "the day of Jesus Christ" or "day of the Lord" (echoing Old Testament prophets).

Most importantly, Paul views these three time dimensions not as isolated frames but as interflowing streams of divine and human activity in which God, Christ, Paul, and the Philippians cooperate to spread the gospel and develop God's "good work in you" day by day until "the

[last] day of Jesus Christ" (Philippians 1:5-6). Good news and works of healing, freeing, caring, and character-forming—call it "salvation" (1:19, 28; 2:12)—are good news and works in "progress" (1:12, 25), not lightning flashes in the pan but built up over time "in any and all circumstances" (4:12) in collaborative partnerships with God and God's people. Continuing cowitnessing and coworking (2:25; 4:3) gets the job done. Such is Paul's big-picture perspective that inspires his thankful faith, hope, and love—in prison, no less.

Intensity: Deep Longing

Emotions can run hot, cold, or lukewarm. Concerning love, for example, it may flame hot as fire, freeze cold as ice, or not move the needle one tick, depending on the context and object of desire. For his part, prisoner Paul is not afraid, lest he appear weak and unmanly, to bare his "hot" heart and express intimate feelings of grateful affection for his Philippians friends. Using an intensive word form, he professes how much "I long [*epipothō*] for all of you" (1:8), as if aching for an absent lover. In the last chapter, Paul addresses the congregation as "my brothers and sisters, whom I love and long for [*epipothētoi*]" (4:1). He also stresses Epaphroditus's deep "longing [*epipothōn*] for all of you" (2:26) while he's away helping Paul on the Philippians' behalf. Absence makes the heart grow not only fonder but also more frustrated, agonized, and heartsick for restored presence.

Reflecting on the five-year anniversary of the COVID-19 crisis, *New York Times* columnist Melissa Kirsch wistfully recalled, "There was so much room for longing in lockdown"[1]—longing for face-to-face contact unfiltered by computer screens, for unfettered opportunities to work and play, for open futures to pursue hopes and dreams. Though not personally afflicted with a deadly disease during his "lockdown," Paul was sharply affected by Epaphroditus's near-fatal illness during his charitable mission to aid Paul. Thankfully, Epaphroditus recovered, sparing Paul "one sorrow after another" (2:25-30). More widely, the locked-up Paul longed intensely for joyful fellowship and fruitful ministry with his Philippian family of faith.

Emotions are felt in our bodies, consciously and unconsciously, in our muscles and tissues, on our skin and hair. From Paul's time to ours, the internal organs of the heart and gut have been regarded as centers of emotional impact. Anxiety can spike heart rate, and grief from a "broken heart" can be devastating, and we're all familiar with gut feelings like nervous butterflies and disgust-triggered retches. Such bodily sensations easily elide into common emotive metaphors like "I love you with all my heart" or "You make me sick to my stomach" (punctuated, if you like, with a heart or nausea emoji).

Paul conveys his deep longing for the beloved Philippians through both cardiac and gastric images: "I hold you in my heart [*kardia*]"; "I long for all of you with the tender affection [*splanchna*] of Christ Jesus" (1:7-8). The latter plural term, politely translated as "tender affection," more literally signifies "guts," "innards," or, as the original KJV puts it, "bowels." ("I long for you with all my bowels" is not advised today in a text message to a lover you'd like to keep.) Paul is not being gross. He's using common language to share his gut feelings of compassionate connection with the Philippians churning in the depths of his being.

Despite his later pullback from "being in need" (4:11), it seems deep down Paul knows he needs his friends' nurturing fellowship to survive. The novelist Sally Rooney has one of her characters confess to another, "I quite literally long to be in your company again."[2] Though "literally" is often used loosely, perhaps Rooney has in mind a literal emotional longing pulsing in the physical heart and gut, akin to what Paul experiences when writing this poignant letter.

Intelligence: Logical Reasoning

The sharp split, long dominating Western thought, between heart and mind, emotion and cognition, *pathos* (passionate feeling) and *logos* (logical reasoning), has been steadily collapsing in recent research across disciplines. The famous meme from the French philosopher René Descartes, "I think, therefore I am," has proven to be short-sighted and single-minded. (Descartes himself knew this, as he also wrote a thoughtful book, *The Passions of the Soul*.) We are not hybrid human–Vulcan creatures like Spock, who fought his human feelings (not always successfully) with pristine Vulcan logic. We are complex thinking–feeling–willing–acting–interacting beings. "I think–feel–will–act–interact"—back and forth, round and round, betwixt and between—"therefore I am *becoming*."

Far from making us unreasonable or anti-intelligent, emotions color our perspectives and judgments about ourselves, others, and the situations we face. The information emotions provide may be pleasant or painful, revealing or distorting. But mental notions are no less variable. So-called *pure reason* is a myth. The fullest, most authentic human lives embrace the mixed, multiplex, messy interplay of hearts and minds.

Aristotle understood long ago that the emotion of "fear makes people inclined to deliberation"[3]—that is, to thinking, evaluating, and appraising. Back to our crooked stick: the initial stab of fear that stops us in our tracks or prompts us to jump away soon sparks closer examination (thinking) and relief (feeling) upon realizing there's no real snake in the grass. Later philosophers, the Stoics in particular, were less appreciative of emotional intelligence than Aristotle, tipping the balance in favor of cool, calm reason, undisturbed by volatile passion. Tranquility above all else at all costs, including the cost of richer relationships, experiences, and insights fueled by the heady mix of passion and reason.

As an educated Hellenistic Jew, Paul was familiar with Greek philosophers and incorporated some of their insights into his Christ-centered worldview. Concerning the value of feeling vis-à-vis thinking, Paul was more in sync with Aristotle than the Stoics: feeling-and-thinking, thinking-and-feeling, a confluence of love-filled hearts and minds more quintessentially Jewish than Greek. "You shall love the LORD your God with all your heart and with all your soul and with all your might" (Deuteronomy 6:5), which Jesus cited in slightly modified form as the greatest commandment of all: "You shall love the Lord your God with all your heart and with all your soul and with all your mind and with all your strength" (Mark 12:29-30). And this God-focused love naturally extends to God's people, including oneself: "You shall love your neighbor as yourself" (Leviticus 19:18; Mark 12:31).

In Philippians, Paul reflects this dynamic thinking-and-feeling, first in thanksgiving for the believers' spiritual development and second in prayer for their moral discernment.

First, Paul reinforces his grateful confidence that God will complete the "good work" of spiritual development in his Philippian gospel partners: "It is right for me to think this way about all of you, because I hold you in my heart" (Philippians 1:7). Notice the tight causal connection between thinking and feeling—to modify Descartes again: *I think because I feel*. In the biblical world, the heart was regarded as the seat of not only feelings but also attitudes, intentions, and expressions ("Out of abundance of the heart the mouth speaks" [Matthew 12:34])—functions that modern science situates in neural brain networks.

Some form of Paul's "think" term (*phroneō*) appears a dozen times in Philippians. I will flag key references in due course. Though the letter is relatively short, Paul does not dash it off the top of his head. He writes deep in thought (with feeling!) about critical issues. Whereas professional scholars might say Paul engages in philosophical analysis or metaphysical theory, spiritual sages might call it contemplative prayer or meditative reflection. Either way, Paul writes from a lively heart and mind suffused with love for God, Christ, all people, and all other creatures (Philippians 2:10-11). It would not be far-fetched to call Philippians a love letter as well as a thank-you letter.

Second, Paul longs for the Philippians' love to sharpen moral discernment of important matters: "This is my prayer, that your love may overflow more and more with knowledge and full insight to help you to determine what really matters" (1:9-10). Emotions signal what matters most to us, what really gets us, grabs us at the gut level, spurring us to deliberate how best to work out these core concerns in our lives. Lord knows, in our current times of overwhelming information and rampant instability, we need to focus our emotional and mental energies on what really matters.

For Paul, like the Old Testament writers and Jesus, nothing matters more to flourishing life than pursuing the "excellent way" of love (1 Corinthians 12:31–13:13); the way of passion, especially compassion, sympathy with sufferers, and the way of reason, especially discerning the most fruitful ways to sow seeds of love that yield a "harvest of righteousness" (Philippians 1:10-11), that does right by other people, that makes right between people, and that rights wrongs of injustice and inequality (see chapter 5). The cheesy Beatles song "All You Need Is Love" gets it basically right. But you also need thoughtful, strategic, active applications of love to make the most difference in a too-often cold and callous world.

Thankful for the Philippians' Participation in Charitable Giving

We've already noted the framing parallel between "I thank [*eucharistō*] my God" (1:3) and "I rejoice [*echarēn*] in the Lord" (Philippians 4:10). Thanksgiving and joy for God, Christ, and the Philippian community are entwined in Paul's attitudes and affections. We come now to see how Paul fleshes out this grateful joy at the end of the letter. Notice the fuller statement: "I rejoice in the Lord greatly that now at last you have revived your concern [*phronein*] for me; indeed, you were concerned [*ephroneite*] for me but had no opportunity to show it" (Philippians 4:10).

Here's that key "think" term (*phroneō*) again, now translated as "concern"—a sincere concern born out of thoughtful consideration for Paul's well-being in his various troubles. It's easy, unfortunately, to sign off a message to someone who's hurting with a cursory, "I'm thinking about you" or "Thoughts and prayers," without thinking much at all—and doing even less. But there's nothing casual or mindless about the Philippians' concern for Paul, as Paul knows from his long relationship with them.

In the present context, Paul especially has in mind their concern for his physical needs, manifested in contributions of money, provisions, and services. But Paul's thinking also betrays a subtle tension between the Philippians' long-standing habit of generosity and a marked interruption in their giving before recently resuming their care for him in prison. While Paul appreciates this "revived" economic concern (4:10), he also hints at his simmering emotional anxiety about the Philippians' temporary lapse in support. He tries to work out these concerns as he winds down the letter.

The Philippians' Generous Contributions

The Philippian church represented the prime model of long-term fiscal backing of Paul's ministry: "You Philippians indeed know that in the early days of the gospel, when I left Macedonia, no church shared with me in the matter of giving and receiving except you alone. For even when I was in Thessalonica, you sent me help for my needs more than once" (4:15-16). This "giving and receiving" partnership focused on the Philippians' giving Paul material resources in grateful response to receiving Paul's ministerial services, a pattern Paul tried to get other congregations to follow: "If we have sown spiritual things among you, is it too much if we harvest material things?" (1 Corinthians 9:11).

Not that Paul demanded payment or sent any bill for services rendered. He's very insistent on not soliciting funds for his personal benefit, lest he appear greedy, self-serving, and exploitative of poor believers who made up the bulk of his parishioners (1 Corinthians 1:26). He worked to support himself as a "tentmaker," crafting cloth and leather goods (Acts 18:1-3). Writing to the Thessalonians, he stressed, "You remember our labor and toil, brothers and sisters; we worked night and day so that we may not burden any of you while we proclaimed to you the gospel of God" (1 Thessalonians 2:9). He viewed this relationship in terms of selfless parental love and responsibility, as mothers and fathers (Paul identifies with both) freely give their "own selves" (2:8) for their children's sake, expecting no remuneration (2:3-12).

Of course, imprisonment cut off Paul's opportunity for paid employment, and whether in or out of jail, he couldn't have worked enough to support himself and the mission partners who traveled with him. So contributions were welcome, provided they were given voluntarily and proportionally according to one's resources. Paul was not beyond using friendly persuasion to encourage giving, but he stopped short of forceful coercion (2 Corinthians 8:3-15; 9:6-15).

In the Philippians' case, not only had they generously supported Paul during his initial visit to Philippi and his current detainment, but they also led the way in contributing to a big collection Paul was organizing. Again, Paul normally avoided fundraising. But this campaign had nothing to do with feathering Paul's own nest; rather, he was collecting funds from the newer gentile-majority congregations to help sustain the very poor Jewish "mother church" in Jerusalem. Though the gentile Christ-fellowships were hardly wealthy themselves, they were generally better off than the Jerusalem group and might have had a few rich donors.

Thanksgiving, again, was a key motivator in this charitable project. Paul was keenly aware that gentiles who came to know and trust Jesus Christ owed a deep debt of gratitude to the Jewish charter fellowship in Jerusalem from which the gospel spread. Paul commented in Romans concerning this collection:

I am going to Jerusalem in a ministry to the saints, for Macedonia and Achaia were pleased to share their resources with the poor among the saints at Jerusalem. They were pleased to do this, and indeed they owe it to them, for if the gentiles have come to share in their spiritual blessings, they ought also to be of service to them in material things.

(Romans 15:25-27).

Prominent among these glad givers were the Christ-communities in Philippi and Thessalonica (Macedonia) and Corinth (Achaia). The Corinthian groups, however, were slower to respond, prompting Paul to urge them to follow through on their pledges. In the process, he used the shrewd tactic of comparing the slacking Corinthians with the model Macedonians. Surely you don't want to be shown up by those northern Philippians and Thessalonians! Paul laid it on pretty thick, accentuating the Macedonians' eager, sacrificial generosity:

We want you [Corinthians] to know... about... the churches of Macedonia, for during a severe ordeal of affliction their abundant joy and their extreme poverty have overflowed in a wealth of generosity on their part. For, as I can testify, they voluntarily gave according to their means and even beyond their means, begging us earnestly for the favor of partnering in this ministry to the saints.

(2 Corinthians 8:1-4; cf. 8:8-14; 9:1-5)

The upshot: If the Macedonians have managed "in their extreme poverty" and "severe ordeal" to give willingly, joyfully, and generously, "even beyond their [limited] means," how much more should you better-off Corinthians, even with your own share of troubles, contribute your fair share to the collection!

In this assessment of Paul's collection, we find an important clue about the history of the Philippian (Macedonian) church. It seems that sometime between its founding by Paul and its sending aid to him in prison, this community experienced a financial crash, plunging it well below the poverty line. Though the Philippians had rebounded enough to resume supporting Paul personally (in addition to contributing to his collection for the Jerusalemites), they were likely still feeling economic pressures when Paul wrote his letter to them, acknowledging their continued "suffering" and "struggle" (Philippians 1:29-30). Money worries may not have been their only problem, but they doubtless caused considerable stress.

Likewise for Paul himself, at least to some extent. Paul makes a valiant attempt to assure the Philippians of God's compassionate care in dire circumstances. But he also seems to need to reassure himself and ease his own anxiety about making ends meet. And I'm glad he did. I, and a lot of other Christians I know, for all our pretensions to live by faith, still struggle with financial worries in a precarious world. Many churches, too, fret about meeting budgets amid shrinking membership and dwindling savings (if they have any left). Let's see how Paul, as he closes this letter, tries to stay thankful, hopeful, and trusting in anxious times.

Paul's Anxious Concerns

Paul provides wise and kind counsel about dealing with anxiety. Classic passages about receiving "the peace of God, which surpasses all understanding" (4:6-7) and being able to "do all things through [Christ] who strengthens me" (4:13) have comforted and encouraged Christians for generations. We will give these texts their due attention in chapter 6. But here we continue to focus on Paul's nettling economic concerns that buck against the peace of God and the strength of Christ.

The lapse in the Philippians' support that Paul alludes to raises two questions that merit further consideration: (1) Why bring up this giving gap when the Philippians have just demonstrated how much they still care for Paul by sending him a personal aide (Epaphroditus) and provisions in prison, and (2) why did the Philippians temporarily stop sending funds and goods to Paul, or to use Paul's delicate language, why did they have "no opportunity" to support him for a season (4:10)? Is there more to this than a steep economic downturn?

First, from his brief remarks, it's hard to know precisely what Paul was thinking and feeling about the Philippians' giving habits. But reading between the lines, his great relief over the Philippians' renewal of aid suggests he's been genuinely worried about his relationship with them and his means of survival, especially in prison when self-employment was cut off. This anxiety is compounded by Paul's strong drive to be self-sufficient, not so much to boost his ego as to bolster his call to serve others, to give rather than to receive. Remember that Paul sees himself as a parent figure responsible for nurturing his children in faith and love. While he joyfully accepts this duty, it causes discomfort when he's the one who needs help, when he becomes dependent on those who've depended on him.

Every parent of adult children knows this feeling. I don't usually pay much attention to TV commercials, but there's one that gets me every time. It's both funny and worrying. I think it's an ad for a credit card, but I don't know which one. It's a restaurant scene where an older couple is dining with their grown son and his wife. When the check comes, both father and son reach for it. They both smile, and the dad eventually lets the son pay. I smile, too, and die a little at the same time. It's hard to let go, even when you're proud and thankful for your children's independence. It's hard to receive when you're used to providing. It's hard to admit you're the one who needs help. I think this is a common feeling (not just for parents), though worse for staunch Stoics and rugged American individualists, especially of the male persuasion.

Paul ties himself in knots. On the one hand, he's grateful for the Philippians' charity: "It was kind of you to share my distress" (Philippians 4:14). "You sent me help for my needs more than once" (4:16). On the other hand, he interlaces these affirmations with protestations: "Not that I am referring to being in need" (4:11). "Not that I seek the gift" (4:17). That's sort of like saying, "Oh you shouldn't have," while quietly conceding, "but I'm glad you did." Or, to adapt Shakespeare, "Methinks Paul doth protest too much."

The fact is, Brother Paul, you do need others' help. You're not self-sufficient, and that's nothing to be ashamed of. No one makes it on their own in the body of Christ, as you yourself know: "God has so arranged the body [of Christ] . . . that . . . the members may have the same care for one another. If one member suffers, all suffer together with it" (1 Corinthians 12:24-26). No one member can say of another, "I have no need of you" (12:21). "Bear one another's burdens, and in this way you will fulfill the law of Christ" (Galatians 6:2). It's not always easy to take your own good advice.

Perhaps, then, by mentioning the Philippians' hiatus in supporting him financially, Paul lets his self-reliant side shade his gratitude. Something like: "You Philippians have been quite generous to me in my current predicament and over the years. But not all the time, to be honest. I managed to survive without your gifts, so I don't really need them. But thanks anyway!"

Admittedly, I'm walking a tightrope here, trying to explain the tightrope Paul walks! I'm not sure I've got it all right. Again, I think Paul is genuinely thankful to the Philippians and not simply using some rhetorical ploy. But I also think he struggles to accept his need for assistance and acknowledge that sometimes it's more blessed—more humble, more human—to receive than to give (reversing Acts 20:35) or, better, to give-and-receive, receive-and-give.

Second, what more might we say about the Philippians' off-and-on financial support for Paul personally and how he felt about the dry period without their funding? We have no sense that the Philippians became disaffected with Paul at any point, perhaps because of his growing reputation as a troublemaker or "pestilent fellow, an agitator," as one Roman lawyer calls him (Acts 24:5). The Philippian believers themselves were no strangers to being suspect characters in the Roman colony where they lived. And this suspicion no doubt had serious economic consequences for the church, as the general Philippi population resisted doing business with devotees of the Lord Jesus Christ (not Lord Caesar), who was executed as an enemy of the Roman state.

Still, as we've seen, even in dire financial straits, the Philippian congregation gave as much as it could—and more—to Paul's collection for poor Jerusalem Jews. Historically, the poor often prove proportionately more generous than the wealthy. But there are limits. You can't give what you don't have. After contributing to the collection, the Philippians would've had little left over to support Paul's personal upkeep. In other words, they lacked the means and opportunity to keep helping Paul. We don't know what suddenly changed to allow them to start helping Paul again, as he now reports from prison. Perhaps a wealthier member joined the church, or the city's business climate became less oppressive. In any case, Paul joyously accepts their charity, even as he chafes against his need for it.

We should also note that, whatever Paul's personal misgivings about needing aid, he in no way chides the Philippians for temporarily stopping their support. He understands their financial struggles and is just as anxious, if not more so, about their well-being. Back to the parental image: You never stop worrying about your kids, no matter how grown-up or well-off they become. And Paul's Philippian family, despite the recent gifts they sent him, is by no means well off. Paul sympathizes with their situation and offers pastoral support.

Fear not, worry not, for "my God will fully satisfy every need of yours according to his riches in glory in Christ Jesus" (Philippians 4:19). Yet another memorable verse in Philippians 4 that has brought comfort and hope to countless Christians in times of need, assuring them of God's unfailing care and share of God's "rich" bounty in Christ Jesus.

But note well: This is a sympathetic blessing offered in the spirit of prayer and thanksgiving (1:3; 4:6)—not a certified check from the Bank of Heaven. It is an invitation to trust, not a trust fund. To use Philippians 4:19 as a prooftext for popular prosperity theology—"God wants you to be rich: Just name it and claim it"—is to misuse Scripture and misunderstand Paul. He's writing from a prison cell, not a penthouse suite, and he's assuring the Philippians that God will meet their needs, not their wants. Moreover, the "rich," abundant life experienced in Christ is a life rich in meaning, in loving relationships that matter most—that money can't buy.

CHAPTER 3

The Struggle in Christ

Key Passages
Philippians 1:18-30
Philippians 2:12-18
Philippians 3:17-21

The theme of suffering is crisply encapsulated in Philippians 1:29-30: " [God] has graciously granted you the privilege [*echaristhē*] not only of believing in Christ but of suffering for him as well, since you are having the same struggle [*agōna*] that you saw I had and now hear that I still have." Several points about this struggle emerge from this text:

- It is a God-granted "privilege," which is to say, another gift to thank God for.
- It is experienced "in Christ" and "for him," per Paul's Christ-centered worldview.
- It is part and parcel of the intimate partnership between Paul and the Philippians: They share "the same struggle" historically and currently.
- It is an intense, agonizing (*agōna*) fight against opponents, like an athletic contest or military conflict.

As far as we know, no Philippian believers had been jailed for their commitment to Christ. But their sympathetic solidarity with Paul would make them feel as if they were bound with him. His struggle, his suffering was theirs and vice versa. A critical part of their shared troubles, remember, was economic. They struggled to make ends meet in a Roman environment that viewed Christ-followers as, at best, strange religious outliers and, at worst, troublesome social destabilizers (recall Paul's disruption of a fortune-telling enterprise in Acts 16:16-24). Even if Christ-confessors did not openly denounce Caesar's rule and continued to attend public events in Roman temples, their devotion to the crucified Jesus Christ as Savior and Lord would have rendered them suspect by mainstream society.

While we have a general sense of Paul and the Philippians' material struggles, we have no detailed dossier of the causes and consequences. They know how they're suffering and who's making their lives difficult without listing offenses and naming names. Paul broadly labels perpetrators as "those opposing you" (Philippians 1:28), "a crooked and perverse generation" (2:15), "dogs" and "evil workers" (3:2), and "enemies of the cross" (3:18). Sounds bad, but who exactly are these bad guys? Paul provides a few clues to their identities, as we will see, but no full profile.

Paul's concern in this letter is less about bemoaning the situation (2:14) and condemning the opposition than about counseling the Philippians on how to live a flourishing life in Christ, whatever the circumstances. But more than that, Paul pushes beyond coping with hardship to cooperating with it as a means of faithful, joyful living. This is the "privilege" dimension of suffering Paul values as a gift from God, which is a hard sell. Unless you're a masochist with a martyr complex, which Paul is not, glib pronouncements of "no pain, no gain" provide cold comfort in the throes of affliction.

In large part, Paul navigates the problem of suffering by feeling, thinking, and acting in between clashing spheres of salvation and destruction, life and death, heaven and earth. Spiritual directors refer to these in-between zones as "thin places," where boundaries blur, thresholds expand, and disparate realms melt into each other. As life inevitably leads to death, so life sprouts anew from death. As the faithful dead are raised to heaven where "our citizenship is" already (3:20), so heavenly reality breaks into earthly existence, as the Lord's Prayer envisions: "May your will be done on earth as it is in heaven" (Matthew 6:10).

Although Paul's perspective is patently spiritual and transcendent, it is not nonphysical. It is thoroughly engaged with human embodiment and emotionality, with flesh and feeling. Paul speaks candidly about living in Christ "always in my body, whether by life or by death" (Philippians 1:20), and being "transform[ed] [from] the body of our humiliation... to the body of [Christ's] glory" (3:21). Notice that suffering bodies are nurtured and rehabilitated, not negated and annihilated.

Likewise, Paul and the Philippians feel a range of conflicting emotional pleasures and pains. Pleasant emotions of joy and peace lighten the pain of suffering (1:3, 25; 4:1, 4-7, 10), as we will unpack in chapter 6. In this chapter, we explore more problematic emotions of fear and shame, the first emotions, as it happens, humans experienced after eating the forbidden fruit: "They knew that they were naked, and they sewed fig leaves together and made loincloths for themselves" (Genesis 3:7). "I was afraid, because I was naked, and I hid myself" (3:10). In Philippians, Paul appraises these primal emotions affecting the circle of life and everything in between.

Living Between Salvation and Destruction

I was raised in a Christian tradition where "being saved" was everything, specifically, being saved from eternal punishment (hell) for my sins through faith in Christ—not through works, God forbid. Jesus was the one and only way to heaven, period. Once we were saved and made eternally secure ("once saved, always saved"), our main mission was to get others saved. We called it "witnessing" or "soul winning."

I bought in early and tried to "win" my childhood friends to Christ. I remember asking a neighborhood buddy one day, "Have you been saved?" Though he went to church (Catholic), he had no clue what I was asking. "Saved from what?" he queried. He lived in the normal world where people or animals might be saved from dangers such as fire, flood, injury, or illness. He couldn't think of any big rescue operations he'd experienced at age nine. Seizing the moment, I proceeded to explain the "plan of salvation" to him in my nine-year-old way. He still didn't get it; thankfully, I dropped the matter, and we stayed friends. At least I tried. I'd done my "good work" of witnessing.

Gradually, I came to realize that biblical "save/salvation" language signifies a broad range of restorative acts, including healing diseases, finding lost ones, rescuing endangered ones, releasing captives, reconciling enemies, and redeeming debts—not just forgiving sins and punching tickets to heaven. Paul's maiden mission in Philippi reported in Acts 16 and his letter to the Philippians illustrate the breadth of Paul's understanding of salvation.

It's worth revisiting two "salvation" cases in Acts 16. First, the fortune-telling slave-girl ironically keeps announcing that Paul and company "proclaim to you the way of salvation" (Acts 16:17). Acts repeatedly identifies the Christ-movement as "the Way" (9:2; 18:25-26; 19:9; 22:4; 24:14, 22), a way of living, not simply believing. What exactly this girl knows about this saving "Way" is anybody's guess, since her speech is influenced by a foreign spirit-agent. But we can be sure she's not thinking of some "plan of salvation" or set of "Four Spiritual Laws" (the hottest gospel tract in my youth). In any event, Paul "saves" her "in the name of Jesus Christ" from enslavement to her spirit-controller, though he does so more out of annoyance, to get her off his back, than benevolence (16:18).

Second, the jailer guarding Paul and Silas fears the capital punishment of his superior officers after an earthquake springs open the prison doors, freeing the inmates. The guard is so distraught that he prepares to kill himself until Paul shouts, "Do not harm yourself, for we are all here" (16:28). This initial "saving" spurs the jailer to ask for more guidance: "Sirs, what must I do to be saved?" (16:30). Clearly, he's focused on being saved from the death penalty for being a bad jailer, not a sinner. Though he might wish the gods would rescue him, he's not suffering a spiritual crisis.

Yet Paul takes this opportunity to expand the man's notion of salvation and connect it to Christ: "Believe in the Lord Jesus, and you will be saved, you and your household" (16:31). The jailer takes Paul and Silas to his house, feeds them, and tends to their wounds, while they further "[speak] the word of the Lord" to him and his household. Everyone accepts the message, is baptized, and becomes a joyful "believer in God" (16:32-34). Not a word is said about sin or hell, forgiveness or heaven. Salvation here involves incorporation into the Christ-community of faith and way of life. Caring for prisoners Paul and Silas—hosting, healing, and feeding them—is a perfect Christlike starting point for this saving journey.

Paul's four "salvation" references in Philippians also reflect a broad frame of thought. Two are embedded in fearful emotional contexts, and the other two in potentially shameful situations.

Paul's Salvation from Shameful Imprisonment

In his present confinement, Paul expresses confidence of a positive outcome, with a tinge of hesitance between knowing and hoping: "I know that... this will turn out for my salvation. It is my eager expectation and hope that I will not be put to shame in any way but that by my speaking with all boldness Christ may be exalted now as always in my body" (Philippians 1:19-20).

Of course, Paul has already begun to walk the path of "salvation" in Christ. But the salvation Paul now seeks is the specific act of release from prison. There's no indication he expects an earthquake this time; a simple judicial release will be fine. Yet Paul's not only concerned about reclaiming his bodily freedom. He's equally concerned about saving his reputation, about not being put to shame. Suffering shame—losing honor, face, standing in the community—is a near-universal human experience, though perhaps more pervasive in Eastern collectivist than Western individualistic societies. Yet Americans are as prone as anyone to cry, "I could just die of shame," following some humiliating *faux pas*. Tragically, these sentiments can become literal self-fulfilling prophecies, as when vulnerable teenagers kill themselves in response to online character assassinations by cruel "friends."

Paul faces a thorny shame dilemma. Even if he's released, acquitted, or pardoned, the fact that he's served jail time potentially taints his reputation. Remember that rival preachers exploited Paul's imprisonment to belittle him and boost their own interests (1:15-17). In the absence of recorded charges, speculation could run rife about what Paul might have done, including misappropriating funds or manipulating donors. Financial fraud, real or trumped-up, is always a good reputation-killer. On the spiritual front, some might have wondered why Paul spent so much time in chains without earthquaking escapes. Is he losing his mojo, becoming increasingly weak, when the tough times demand a swaggering strongman? Has he lost favor with God and Christ?

Obviously, Paul could defend himself more effectively if he were out of prison. Yet even in jail, Paul buoys his hope of release (salvation) by three means: the Philippians' prayers, Christ's Spirit, and Paul's bold witness to Christ. As much as Paul appreciates the Philippians' material gifts, he covets their prayers even more as a channel of the "Spirit of Jesus Christ" (1:19). The robust "partnership in the Spirit" (2:1) enjoyed by Paul and the Philippian congregation mutually sustains and "saves" them. It also motivates Paul's bold witness to the saving Christ before the imperial guards. Their attentiveness to the gospel (1:13; 4:22) cannot help but bolster Paul's hope of being released.

Yet Paul makes no pretense of his own powers of persuasion or salvation. Whether in prison or not, his ministerial philosophy remains remarkably humble:

> *I decided to know nothing among you except Jesus Christ and him crucified. And I came to you in weakness and in fear and in much trembling. My speech and my proclamation were made not with persuasive words of [human] wisdom but with a demonstration of the Spirit and. . . the power of God.*
>
> *(1 Corinthians 2:2-5)*

The Philippians' Salvation from Fearsome Opponents

Paul speaks openly about his predicament not to vent or elicit sympathy but to help "save" his struggling Philippian brothers and sisters in Christ. No armchair counselor, Paul speaks from experience and empathy, from a vital connection between "my salvation" (Philippians 1:19) and "your salvation" (1:28).

Paul shifts the emotional focus from shame to fear of "those opposing you" and impeding "your salvation" (1:28). He names no opposition party, and we should not imagine some counter-Christ branch of a Roman intelligence agency in Philippi. The Christ-community was neither big nor bad enough to warrant that much concern. But as a strange minority group devoted to a crucified Messiah, the misfitted fellowship would have found itself variously slighted, snubbed, and short-changed by the wider public. A scary situation.

Yet Paul urges his Philippian friends not to succumb to fear but to surmount it, "in no way being frightened by those opposing you"; such a confident attitude certifies "your salvation" and signals "their destruction" (1:28). As "salvation" is shorthand for the right way of life, so "destruction" marks the off-road to ruin. Paul does not envision some shock-and-awe wipeout of the Roman colony and violent takeover by Christ's followers (as if they could). Paul advocates loving your enemies, as Jesus does (Matthew 5:39-42; Luke 6:27-36; Romans 12:14-21). The destruction of formidable Christ-resisting forces, then, is ultimately self-destruction. They may be open for booming business on the Egnatian Way, but they bar themselves from the true way of salvation.

Nice words, Paul. Fear not: Your staunch faith in Christ will save you and stop your foes. But warning against fear implies that fear can be thwarted by a decisive act of will. Easier said than done. Fear resists easy management. Will resolving to be "in no way frightened" (Philippians 1:28) by forceful opposition automatically save us from food shortages, shabby housing, poor health conditions, and other struggles endemic to our marginal status in Philippi? How do we work through our fear toward practical salvation here and now?

In short, here's Paul's fear-reducing, salvation-producing advice: Work together as one—with God. Keep "standing firm in one spirit, striving side by side with one mind for the faith of the gospel" (1:27). One spirit, one mind. The "spirit" can refer both to the "Spirit of Jesus Christ" (1:19) and to the congregation's collective spirit. One "mind" does not mean total agreement in thought but rather a deep psychological bond and common aim. Moreover, this dynamic spirit–mind network is suffused with divine power and purpose: "This is God's doing" (1:28).

The Philippians' Salvation Through Fearful Cooperation with God

Paul emphasizes the cooperative work of salvation between God and God's people: "Work on your own salvation... for it is God who is at work in you... both to will and to work for his good pleasure" (2:12-13). As usual in this letter, the "you" pronouns are plural: The Philippian congregation must work together with one another and with God to accomplish God's whole-making mission. Clearly, Paul is not allergic to good works of salvation, in tandem with faith. Such works do not earn God's favor, which is freely given, but they do evidence obedience to God's will (2:8, 12) and the inner workings of God's grace. Though the Protestant tradition has often pitted Paul's gospel against the message of James, the Paul of Philippians would readily "Amen" James's dictum that "faith by itself, if it has no works, is dead" (James 2:17; cf. 2:14-26; Ephesians 2:8-10).

But there's more. You may have noticed I left something out of Philippians 2:12. It's only a short phrase, but it's a shocker. The full statement reads, "Work on your own salvation *with fear and trembling*" (emphasis added). We might prefer to omit this additional phrase! But there it is, and the Greek sentence places "with fear and trembling" first for emphasis, so we don't miss this key emotional component.

But wait a minute. I thought Paul was trying to calm and encourage the anxious Philippians. In the present text, Paul doesn't specify who or what they should engage "with fear and trembling"; but it's unlikely he suddenly shifts gears and advises, "On second thought, you best be very afraid of your enemies and not rile them up if you want to be saved." Though no naïve denialist about pain and suffering, Paul is no cowering defeatist either. Remember, he speaks, writes, and acts "with all boldness," even in prison (1:20).

So, who or what should the Philippians fear and tremble at? Surrounding the fear-and-trembling text in Philippians 2:12 are references to "God the Father" (2:11) and "God who is at work in you" (2:13). Thus, Paul appears to be calling the Philippians to *fear God*. This a familiar biblical concept but one, I'm afraid, that's often misunderstood.

Many modern folk have a problem with ancient notions of fearing a frightful God poised to zap us when we get out of line. Instead, they prefer to translate old-style fear-talk concerning God into more positive language of praising and worshipping God with all due awe, reverence, and honor. In contemporary worship lingo, "Our God is an Awesome God." Well, yes, that tracks. And happy worship certainly plays better than a horror show. But it's not the whole game. There's no special term in the Bible for "reverent fear" set apart from other forms of fear. "Awesome" aspects of fearing God complement but do not replace more terrifying, truly fearful, dimensions. Biblical fear of God remains inherently fearsome, as Paul makes clear by linking "fear" with "trembling" (2:12). While we may prefer glad tidings of comfort and joy over hard calls to fearful and tremulous work with God, Paul's gospel blends both elements.

Yet granting a fearsome element to God's character by no means makes God a monster. That's twisting an "awesome" God into an "awful" scary force, more demonic than divine. I'm reminded of an episode of the popular TV comedy, *Everybody Loves Raymond*. Raymond's brother, Robert, has been seeing a woman named Amy and wants to marry her. But when Robert visits Amy's tight-laced religious parents to ask for their blessing, things become awkward. Trying to make a good impression, Robert brings Raymond along as a character witness. Raymond has a successful career, a wonderful wife, and two lovely children—"a good, good family," Robert says, but then prattles on, "God-fearing, right? Church every Sunday. All of us, God-fearing people. We're scared to death!"[1]

To be sure, the New Testament provides ready grist for the mill of fire-and-brimstone sermons in statements like, "It is a fearful thing to fall into the hands of the living God" (Hebrews 10:31) and "For indeed our God is a consuming fire" (12:29). But there's also a strong counter strain stressing God's fear-dispelling love: "God is love" and "There is no fear in love, but perfect love casts out fear; for fear has to do with punishment" (1 John 4:16, 18).

What is Paul's perspective? He has his share of warnings about God's wrath and fiery end-time judgment (Romans 1:18; 2:5; 1 Corinthians 3:13-15; 1 Thessalonians 1:9-10). But not in Philippians. Here he speaks vaguely of opponents' "destruction," as we've seen, but without laboring the point. His primary interest is in his and the Philippians' salvation, not in their enemies' elimination.

Also, Paul doesn't specify what the Philippians should fear about God. There's no accompanying threat of punishment. No "Work hard or else!" Remember, God is faithfully working "in you" for salvation (Philippians 2:13). So, again, we wonder, what does God-directed fear and trembling have to do with salvation? I wish Paul had said more here. I can live with a degree of tension between the wondrous and wrathful God. There are evils and injustices in the world that demand righteous, angry responses. But a tyrant who conditions salvation on forced obedience and fearful submission is not worthy of the divine name and not deserving of worship.

The Greek philosopher Aristotle offers insights about fear that may help us understand Paul's view. Consider two points. First, a connection between fear and hope. Aristotle states, "Some hope of salvation must endure concerning the matter over which [people] anxiously contend. For fear renders people apt to deliberate, yet no one deliberates about hopeless things."[2] Though fearfulness and hopefulness seem like strange bedfellows, Aristotle makes an intriguing observation: Fear makes you "deliberate" or, more simply, think; fear kick-starts thinking about what you can do in a precarious environment to ensure your well-being. In Paul's terms, fear motivates you to think about how you might cowork on your salvation with the wonderful, fearful God of immeasurable love and power. Crucially, fear counters despair. Whereas hopeless despair paralyzes, hopeful fear energizes saving work. Fear lets you know you're alive and want to stay that way!

Second, Aristotle connects fear and humility via pity: "Frightening things are all those that elicit pity, when they happen to others or are about to happen."[3] Again, at first blush, fear and pity seem miles apart. But it makes sense that when we see others in a pitiful state—like suffering a terrible illness or financial collapse—our concern for them often boomerangs as fear that we, too, as fellow fragile creatures, might suffer similar dreadful fates. But, again, fear may prove useful, in this case evoking humility. As Paul writes in Romans, humans share a common creatureliness "subjected to futility" and "groaning together" in pain and suffering; yet "in hope we were saved" (Romans 8:18-24)—that is, hope linked to humble acknowledgment of our need for help. We can only hope to save ourselves as we humbly work and strive together with "God, who is at work in you, enabling you both to will and to work for his good pleasure" (Philippians 2:13).

Paul and the Philippians' Salvation from Shameful Enemies of the Cross

Along with managing his own potential shame as a prisoner, Paul exposes the palpable shame of "many" opponents who continue to "live as enemies of the cross" (3:18). These antagonists don't appear to be attacking Christ, Paul, or the Philippian congregation directly; rather, it's something about their lifestyle that undermines Christ's cross. A bedrock tenet of Paul's gospel is that, strange as it may seem, Christ's crucifixion empowers God's salvation: "To us who are being saved, it [the message about the cross] is the power of God" (1 Corinthians 1:18). Something, then, about these enemies' conduct is tempting Christ-believers to stray from the crossway of salvation.

The only behavioral clues Paul provides about these opponents are that "their god is the belly, and their glory is in their shame; their minds are set on earthly things" (Philippians 3:19). In other words, they're a bunch of self-indulgent, shame-reveling "belly"-servers obsessed with "earthly" status and possessions. By stark contrast, the cross of Christ marks the way of self-emptying, humble, saving service to humanity (2:6-8), not least the least glorious and glamorous among us.

Living the high life has its allure, of course. Who among us in Western society has not coveted richer food, finer clothes, fancier cars, and a host of other glittery goods and services? Though we might sing of "The Old Rugged Cross," most Christians (including me) are not looking to carry a rougher cross. We've already got more than we can handle on our metaphorical plates, partly from striving to stack all the goodies we can on our literal plates.

To the extent the Philippian believers felt their commitment to the crucified Christ was hurting their standing in the wider community, they might have been tempted to tone down their cross talk and walk. If they wore cross necklaces back then, they might have done so cautiously: nothing too flashy and hanging loose enough to tuck the cross part inside their tunics in public settings. Or maybe (probably) I'm projecting my wary sentiments. In any event, Paul assures his friends that Christ's salvation will prevail against opposing forces.

Consider three points: First, Paul asserts concerning "enemies of the cross" that "their end is destruction" (3:19), as he said earlier about "those opposing you" (1:28). Again, Paul views their "destruction" as self-induced by their belly-driven lifestyles. Their consumerist obsession will ultimately consume them. This point fits a raft of modern studies showing that extreme wealth and conspicuous consumption by no means guarantee satisfaction and may lead to depression and dysfunction.

Second, Jesus's crucifixion was not the end for Jesus but instead a vital revelation in itself (not only because of resurrection) of God's salvation, especially to those exploited by ruthless rulers. In a reverse tour de force, God used the cross—the quintessential instrument of Roman death-dealing dominance—to save the weakest, the lowliest, the most despised by the supposed smart set and strongmen and to shame pretenders to wisdom and power (1 Corinthians 1:17-28). What's more is that Paul and the Philippian believers, in whom God's saving work has begun (Philippians 1:6), are "expecting a Savior, the Lord Jesus Christ"—the crucified, exalted Christ—to complete this saving work when he returns (3:20-21).

Third, Paul makes a stunning point about citizenship. While many Christ-confessors might be treated as second-class citizens or denied Roman citizenship in Philippi, they now hold a greater and higher citizenship in the heavenly realm (3:20)! I will explore this amazing identity more fully when we discuss living between heaven and earth.

Living Between Life and Death

The imprisoned Paul speaks candidly in Philippians about his immediate life-and-death struggle. While his readers could take much wisdom and comfort from his testimony, their own struggles, difficult in their own ways, do not appear to include imminent threats of physical punishment by the Roman government. But Paul faces a real possibility of execution as a condemned criminal.

How does Paul cope with this cliff-edge scenario? Amazingly, he transforms this scary space into a "thin place," a promising portal between death and life. Sounds good—almost too good to be true. Is Paul's mind starting to crack under duress, causing him to indulge in wild, wishful fantasies? But he's not ranting or raving in this letter. He calmly presents the core convictions that drive his confident perspective. I focus here on Philippians 1:20-26 and 2:17-18, beginning with what we might call Paul's two-part life motto: "For to me [1] living is Christ and [2] dying is gain" (1:21).

Living Is Christ

Paul bundles the prepositional array of life in/for/of/with/through Christ into the sweeping declaration: "Living is Christ" (1:21). Actually, Paul doesn't use the Greek "be" verb here. He says it all in two words: "To-be-living / Christ" (*zēn Christos*), which intensifies the Living/ Christ connection. We might signify this interlink as "Living = Christ" or, better, "Living ↔ Christ."

This is no abstract doctrine for Paul but rather a deeply personal conviction based on lived experience "in Christ" (plus the other prepositions). "For me," Paul emphasizes, "living is Christ," period (1:21). Moreover, Paul's Christ-centered motto is no Christ meme he happened to pick up and parrot but rather a dynamic relational union "with Christ" (plus the other prepositions). Further, this vibrant fellowship between Paul and Christ, for all its elements of wonder and mystery, is not purely mystical and certainly not magical make-believe. In fact, it's thoroughly practical, worked out in the process of day-to-day living. Or to use a philosophical term, Paul's bond with Christ is profoundly existential, touching the core of his being and affecting the full arc of life-and-death experience.

Far from dismissing Christ's death, Paul embraces the cross as the saving "power of God" (1 Corinthians 1:18), as evidenced by Christ's bodily resurrection and by Paul's vital sense of Christ's animating presence with him on the precipice of his own execution. Such absorption in the living Christ inspires Paul's boldness to honor Christ "now as always in my body, whether by life or by death" (Philippians 1:20).

It also motivates Paul's surprising joy amid his ominous ordeal. Perhaps his prison sentence will end in death. If so, Paul imagines this death as a sacrificial offering to God on the Philippians' behalf: "Even if I am poured out like a drink offering upon the altar of service for your faith, I am glad. I'm glad with all of you" (2:17, CEB). This image evokes Christ's outpouring of blood for the salvation of "many," as memorialized in the Lord's Supper (Mark 14:24; 1 Corinthians 11:25-26). The saving, life-giving work of Christ, far from being stanched by death, streams through and out of death into new life. A reason to rejoice, indeed!

But Paul has more to say about death "benefits" in the second part of his motto.

Dying Is Gain

We might expect a more modest corollary to "Living is Christ"—like "Dying is not final"—than "Dying is gain" (Philippians 1:21). The economic term Paul uses seems to give dying a lot of credit. Accepting death as inevitable and transformable is one thing; assessing death as profitable and valuable is quite another.

No doubt Paul is speaking metaphorically about postmortem rewards. However marvelous heaven might be, the Bible provides no satellite imaging of its environs, which is to say, I'm not holding much hope for actual mansions, golden streets, crystal waters, jeweled crowns, or other treasures. I will say more about heaven later, but for now, let's agree that Paul scarcely views heaven as a five-star resort. Yet his use of "gain" suggests he regards death as a good thing. If that's not shocking enough, he muses that death may be a better thing, "far better" in fact than staying alive (1:23). As Eugene Peterson's *The Message* paraphrases, "Some days I can think of nothing better."

We might wonder again about Paul's sanity. Is he losing his grip on life, perhaps even considering suicide as a "far better" option than languishing in prison or suffering state execution? Highly doubtful. Paul's prison struggles are very real and arduous, but he's no quitter. He's not looking for an escape hatch. He remains wholeheartedly in love with life, whatever the circumstances, because all life is worth living in Christ, whose essence is living!

So, what's Paul got to gain from death? In a nutshell: More Christ! More Christ-Life! More living with Christ. What is "far better" about death is the opportunity "to depart and be with Christ" (1:23) more intimately. Of course, Paul is already spiritually with Christ now as Christ abides with him in jail. Prison bars are no barrier for the living Christ. But Paul anticipates more direct and intense participation in death and resurrection with Christ (see 3:7-11).

As it happens, Paul says nothing in Philippians about going to heaven, being relieved of all suffering, enjoying freedom in paradise, or reuniting with deceased loved ones. Not that he would deny these benefits, but Paul's overriding philosophy of afterlife is that it simply leads to a more dynamic Christ-life. Paul sees more of a life–death continuum than a disconnect. He's learned to live in the "thin places" between life and death. The "Thin Zone," we might call it, after Rod

Serling's pioneering TV series *The Twilight Zone*, except that instead of an eerie *noir* vibe, Paul envisions more of a "Highlight Zone" joyously illumined by the living Christ.

In another sense, Paul seems to view life-or-death matters as fortunate coin flips in which he's "a winner either way," as Mary Chapin Carpenter croons in her bouncy ballad "I Feel Lucky."[4] In a cheeky move, Paul suggests that he has a hard, yet happy, choice between life and death: "I cannot say which I will choose. I am hard pressed between the two"—between living and dying (1:22-23). Hmm. Is this Paul's choice to make?

Choosing Between Life and Death

Like all of us, Paul has the power to choose how he thinks and feels about life and death. But his apparent claim to choose whether he lives or dies exceeds human capacity (except in extreme situations of self-inflicted or assisted suicide). We all know that we will die someday, but none of us knows when. In a traditional view of providence that Paul typically endorses, our fates are in God's hands. But here, Paul seems engaged in rhetorical musing as if he controlled his destiny.

But Paul's not playing mind games. Rather, he's conducting a meaningful thought experiment about the critical fork in the road he's facing: one path leading to execution, the other to release. Paul can accept either course as God-graced: one leading to a "better" life "with Christ" and the other to more "fruitful work for Christ" (1:22-23, NLT). Paul also affirms one option as optimal for the Philippians: "To remain in the flesh is more necessary for you. Since I'm convinced of this, I know that I will remain and continue with all of you for your progress and joy in the faith" (1:24-25). Significantly, Paul prioritizes present earthly work over afterlife ease. Or in "thin" terms, earthly and heavenly ministry converge.

Of course, Paul cannot absolutely know he will be set free and allowed to visit Philippi. A couple can put money down on a Mediterranean cruise and make plans accordingly, but they can't know for sure those plans will pan out (best to purchase cancellation insurance). Still, in an uncertain world, Paul decides to choose life and to pursue lifesaving goals as the most fruitful way to follow Christ.

This dynamic philosophy of life shines through a breathtaking passage in Deuteronomy, attributed to Moses as he prepares the travel-weary Israelites to enter the Promised Land. Paul cites part of this text in Romans 10:5-8. I wouldn't be surprised if he also had it in mind when writing Philippians:

> *"Surely, this commandment that I am commanding you today is not too hard for you, nor is it too far away. It is not in heaven, that you should say, 'Who will go up to heaven for us and get it for us so that we may hear it and observe it?'... No, the word is very near to you; it is in your mouth and in your heart for you to observe....*
>
> *I call heaven and earth to witness against you today that I have set before you life and death, blessings and curses. Choose life so that you and your descendants may live."*
>
> *(Deuteronomy 30:11-12, 14, 19)*

Living Between Heaven and Earth

Moses's life-choosing summons before personified witnesses of "heaven and earth," as if in a cosmic courtroom, reveals a critical dimension of God's universe that is often missed. I know I missed it for years, though it should have been obvious from the Bible's first verse: "In the beginning God created the heavens and the earth" (Genesis 1:1, NIV). Note the heaven(s) and earth—both spheres are created by God. Biblical cosmology views the universe as united by its Creator. Intriguingly, the vast, expansive multiverse of modern physics also adopts an intricately interlinked global and galactic worldview, with or without God.

Living in an Interlinked Cosmos

For Paul, of course, everything exists through God and Christ: "For us there is one God, the Father, from whom are all things and for whom we exist, and one Lord, Jesus Christ, through whom are all things and through whom we exist" (1 Corinthians 8:6). And "all things" aligning under God and Christ include heaven and earth in synergy—working together, not separately. Like many Christians, I was raised to view heaven "up there" and earth "down here" as opposing realms, good versus evil, perfect versus flawed, divine versus human.

Yes, the earthly sector is subject to flaws and frailties, not least because of its wayward human inhabitants, while in the heavenly arena God's goodwill is perfectly realized. But the two realms are not sealed off from one another or set apart by unfathomable distance. There's plenty of porous "space" between "heaven" and "earth" where the divine and human meet, especially per Paul, in the person of Christ, the embodiment of God the Creator and Sustainer of the cosmos. Everything comes together "in Christ" (see Philippians 2:5-11; discussed in chapter 4).

This universal Christ-factor is better imagined as a cyclical stream than a vertical chain, as swirling together than stacked top to bottom. An up–down orientation is hard to shake, however, for us nonphysicists. One vertical image I've found helpful is Jacob's ladder. On the run from his furious brother Esau, Jacob sleeps one night under the stars and dreams of a "ladder" (KJV), more accurately a "stairway" stretching from earth to heaven (cue Led Zeppelin), with God standing at the earthly base and a host of angels zipping up and down, assuring Jacob of divine protection. Upon waking, Jacob calls the place Bethel, "House of God" (Genesis 28:10-22).

In John's Gospel, Jesus evokes this ladder image in a solemn statement to a new believer named Nathanael: "Very truly, I tell you, you will see heaven opened and the angels of God ascending and descending upon the Son of Man" (John 1:51). "Son of Man/Humankind" is Jesus's favorite self-designation. He himself is the dual-direction moving stairway linking earth and heaven. Imagining a cosmic ladder in perpetual motion makes me dizzy, but I like the feeling.

Living in a Citizen-Marked Country

Linked to Paul's vision of cosmic connectivity (the World Wide Web) is his approach to citizenship. Few issues of social identity are as critical as citizenship, which confers legal rights within established borders to some people (citizens) and not others (aliens). It remains a hotly contested issue in many countries.

In the Roman Empire, citizenship was a highly prized status enjoyed only by a minority. Most subjects, including slaves and most immigrants and nonethnic Romans, were not citizens. A path to citizenship was available but costly. Remember that Acts makes a big deal of Paul's citizenship, starting with his illegal arrest and imprisonment in Philippi without due process. After the earthquake jailbreak, Paul plays the citizenship card with relish: "They have beaten us in public, uncondemned, men who are Romans [citizens], and have thrown us into prison, and now they are going to discharge us in secret? Certainly not! Let them come and take us out themselves"—with an apology (Acts 16:37-38). Later, when he's arrested in Jerusalem, Paul announces that he's a Greek-speaking Jew from Tarsus with Roman citizenship from birth, in contrast with a Roman officer named Claudius Lysias, who tells Paul, "It cost me a large sum of money to get my citizenship" (21:37–22:3, 25-29).

Curiously, however, Paul never mentions his Roman citizenship in his letters, raising the possibility that Acts embellishes Paul's résumé for political effect. But Paul has no cause to show his citizenship papers to church audiences, most of whom were noncitizens. Yet in Philippians, Paul intriguingly alludes to all believers' citizenship in two overlapping realms: as citizens of the world (Philippians 1:27) and citizens of heaven (3:20).

Living as Good Citizens of the World

As Paul shifts from reflecting on his personal suffering to addressing the Philippians' similar struggles, he urges them to "live your life in a manner worthy of the gospel of Christ" (1:27). They couldn't control outsiders' derisive attitudes and actions toward them, but they could control how they conduct themselves as followers of Christ. In this way, they both commend Christ's life-giving way to their opponents and shore up their own confidence in God's joyous salvation (1:27-28). Paul's strategy for dealing with oppressors centers on faithful Christlike living, not forceful counterattack.

More specifically, the verb rendered "live your life" (*politeuesthe*) implies "political" engagement in a "city" (*polis*): living your life as a citizen. What a provocative challenge for lowly, noncitizen Christ-followers in Roman Philippi! How can they "live as citizens" in this city? Only by changing the realm and aim of citizenship.

Though Paul does not advocate anti-Roman revolution, neither does he bend over backward to accommodate Roman civic interests. The "citizen" life Paul calls believers to live is not a life loyal to Rome but a life "worthy of the gospel of Christ," evidenced in "striving side by side with one mind for the faith of the gospel" (1:27). It swears and shows united allegiance to Christ's gospel by faith.

Note two key watchwords: "gospel" (*euangelion*) and "faith" (*pistis*), both with definite articles "the." The gospel is not a manifesto marking insular nationalist boundaries but rather an open message of Christ's saving good news for the whole world. And the faith does not constitute a governmental agenda or set of beliefs and laws but rather a loving, trusting, living, working relationship with Christ—being faithful to and with Christ (and partner disciples) in heart, mind, and conduct. Such Christ-centered "citizen" action is good news for Paul and the

Philippian congregation, joining them in common cause, supporting them in similar struggles, and assuring them of God's salvation. And not incidentally, it's also good news for the city of Philippi, the Roman Empire, and all places and peoples enfolded in God's gracious love.

Living as Graced Citizens of Heaven Now

I promised to return to Paul's remarkable claim to heavenly citizenship. Well, here we are. In contrast to "enemies of the cross of Christ" preoccupied with "earthly things" without regard for their divine Creator's good designs, "our citizenship is in heaven" (3:18-20). Paul does not stress going to heaven after death or after Christ's return, as if believers' tickets are punched and passports stamped for a distant paradise. Instead, Paul affirms being in the heavenly realm here and now, already possessing and enjoying heavenly citizenship, irrespective of Roman status.

To be sure, Paul expects "the Lord Jesus Christ" to return "from" this heavenly realm to "transform the body of our humiliation"—that is, our natural bodies subject to pain and suffering—into the image of Christ's glorious, resurrected body (3:20-21). But again, Paul says nothing about Christ snatching us away from earth and whisking us to heaven. More likely, Paul envisions Christ extending the influence of God's perfect heaven-sphere into the imperfect earthly environment. The ultimate goal is not only to revitalize human bodies but also to renovate the cosmos. "In Christ, there is a new creation" (2 Corinthians 5:17), the genesis of "new heavens and a new earth" (Isaiah 65:17).

We keep coming back to the open, "thin" borders of God's creation, in this case between heavenly and earthly "citizens" in an evolving universe. This wide worldview is reinforced in Ephesians. While some scholars dispute Paul's direct authorship of this letter, it resonates with much of Paul's writing, including his thoughts about salvation and heavenly citizenship in Christ: "By [God's] grace you have been saved—and raised . . . up with [Christ] and seated . . . with [God] in the heavenly places in Christ Jesus" (Ephesians 2:5-6). "So then, you are no longer strangers and aliens, but you are fellow citizens (*sympolitai*) with the saints and also members of the household of God" (2:19; cf. 1:9-10). Amazingly, in this view, amid earthly strife and struggles, Christ's people enjoy two extraordinary benefits: a safe place in God's heavenly "house" as a present reality, not simply as a future reservation, and a permanent status as full-fledged "citizens" in God's commonwealth, not simply "dreamers."

This is heady stuff, too mystical by half, you might say. But it's worth stretching our minds to absorb what we can and grow into fuller knowledge and insight (Philippians 1:9). Beyond that, it's important to note Paul's emphasis on practical living. Paul by no means encourages retreating from a troubled world and relaxing in cushy heavenly "seats." Rather, he implores countering those who "live as enemies" of the crucified Christ with better living on earth as faithful citizens of heaven: "Brothers and sisters, join in imitating me, and observe those who live according to the example you have in us" (3:17)—and, above all, in Christ—whose life story we now consider more fully.

CHAPTER 4

The Story of Christ

Key Passages
Philippians 2:1-30
Philippians 3:17–4:1

If anything has become clear so far in our Philippians study, it's that Paul's secret of life starts and ends with Christ: "Living is Christ" (1:21). Given this Christ-centered perspective, however, it's surprising how rarely Paul refers to Jesus's earthly life and ministry. If all we had were Paul's letters (no Gospel narratives), we'd know next to nothing about Jesus of Nazareth beyond the fact he "was born of a woman" (Galatians 4:4), died on a cross, and was raised from the dead. To be sure, Paul regards Jesus's crucifixion and resurrection as the most significant saving events in world history, but he largely overlooks the thirty years or so prior to these events.

Paul was not a Jesus biographer or historian. He wrote letters to Christ-confessing congregations in the heat of the moment, addressing pressing issues and situations. He also no doubt assumed some common knowledge about Jesus's life. But we should not also assume Paul had little interest in Jesus's life story. While he is shy on biographical details, Paul places Jesus's earthly life within the panoramic scope of his eternal life. He takes a wide-lens, big-picture view of Jesus's whole career, stretching back before Jesus's incarnation on earth and beyond his crucifixion and resurrection.

Nowhere is this clearer than in Philippians, where, amid his personal and pastoral reflections, Paul interjects a short but sweeping poetic story of Jesus Christ (2:6-11). This piece has the form and feel of a hymn, a Jesus song, perhaps one of the earliest in Christian worship. Fast forward to the Jesus-people of the 1970s, and this ancient song became the basis of a popular chorus, "He Is Lord," which I regularly sang and played on the guitar as a youth minister.

Scholars debate whether the Philippians Christ-hymn was composed or adapted by Paul; either way, Paul embraces it as an inspired précis of the cosmic Christ-story. But Paul does not only offer this song in praise to God and Christ. Once again, he's concerned about believers' practice of following Christ's example, living like Christ, and embodying Christ's full mindset. Introducing the hymn, Paul stresses the message more than the music: "Let the same mind[set] be in you that was in Christ Jesus" (2:5). Sing it, brothers and sisters, so you can live it in Christ!

The Extraordinary Love Story of Christ

A memorable song both informs and inspires, stirring mind and heart through its lyrics and lilt. The Christ-hymn in Philippians 2:6-11 is a compact love story of Christ set to song. To catch the hymn's rich meaning, it's important to slow the tempo and carefully track its movements. I segment it into four stanzas corresponding to major stages of Christ's story, all parts meshing together like a fine-tuned gospel quartet: (1) preexistence (2:6), (2) self-emptying (2:7), (3) cross-execution (2:8), and (4) high exaltation (2:9-11).

Christ's Preexistence

Preexistence seems like a strange term. How can you exist before you exist? In some ethereal green room before making your grand entrance into the world in your mother's womb? Or in more religious terms, preexisting in the eternal mind of God or as another creature in a cycle of reincarnation, which presumes preincarnation? Fun to muse about but hard to prove, and neither divine imagination nor preincarnation quite fits the Philippians Christ-hymn.

Still, for lack of a better term, *preexistence* is how Christian theologians refer to Jesus Christ's existence in a different "form" prior to becoming a human being. As wonderful as the Gospels' Christmas story is, with banner moments of Jesus's Spirit-conception in Mary's womb, birth in Bethlehem, and bedding in a manger, this is not the beginning of Christ's life—at least not for Paul. He never mentions Jesus's virginal conception or his Bethlehem birthplace. Instead, Paul highlights Christ's eternal life from before the creation of the world.

To repeat Paul's declaration in 1 Corinthians 8:6: "There is . . . one Lord, Jesus Christ, through whom are all things and through whom we exist." The existence of all creatures owes to Christ's preexisting creative love and power. Paul expands on this point in another hymn-style text:

> *[Christ] is the image of the invisible God, the firstborn of all creation, for in him all things in heaven and on earth were created, things visible and invisible, whether thrones or dominions or rulers or powers—all things have been created through and for him. He himself is before all things, and in him all things hold together.*
>
> *(Colossians 1:15-17)*

Here Christ's "birth" is envisioned as a "firstborn" re-producing of God's self, in turn generating "all things in heaven and on earth."

At the outset of the Philippians hymn, however, Paul does not focus on Christ's primeval involvement in creating the world. Rather, he stresses Christ's intimate and consummate relationship with God: being "in the form of God," in God's "nature" or "image," enjoying full "equality with God" (Philippians 2:6). But here's the stunner: Christ "did not regard" this divine equality "as something to be grasped." What does that mean? That's a hard concept to grasp!

Consider two possibilities. First, Christ did not need to take hold of equality with God because he already had this identity, freely shared with the loving God. Since Christ had received from God this perfect God-"form" and God-fellowship, he did not need to reach for it. In this respect, Christ contrasts with the first humans who outstretched their created natures by grasping for the forbidden "fruit" of total Godlikeness, as if to make themselves independent deities instead of graced beneficiaries of the "image of God" (Genesis 1:26-27; 3:1-7; see Romans 5:12-21; 1 Corinthians 15:42-49 for Paul's reflections on Christ and Adam).

Second, and more central to the Philippian hymn's movement, Christ did not need to keep hold of equality with God that he already possessed. In other words, he did not clutch or cling to his divine identity as if it were a fragile, breakable bond. Christ remains thoroughly secure in his relationship with God, which also means he doesn't need to strut or flaunt it before other would-be "dominions and rulers and powers" (Colossians 1:16). Here the implied contrast is not so much with Adam as with Caesar, who constantly promoted his divine "Augustness" with military parades, executionary spectacles (like crucifixions), monetary media (coins embossed with his image), statuary monuments, and honorary temples. Such self-boosterism betrays an underlying fear of losing face and favor.

Christ has no such fear. Thus, he's willing to alter his status if his love for God, humanity, and all creation demands it. And it does, as the next stanza reveals.

Christ's Self-Emptying

In a shocking shift, modulating to a lower key, the Philippian hymn announces that the eternal Christ "emptied himself" and took on a different "form" (2:7). Two critical questions arise: What new "form" did Christ assume? What did Christ empty himself of and why?

The text describes Christ's transformation in three closely related phrases:

- Taking the form of a slave
- Assuming human likeness
- Being found in appearance as a human

The divine Christ became a human being. Such god-man stories were common in the Greco-Roman world, and Jewish tradition had its share of divine-messenger angels appearing on earth in human form. But these analogies miss a central feature of Christ's portrait, namely, his death by execution highlighted in the next verse (2:8). Deities and angels don't die, with or without human "forms." Further, Paul is wary of misguided attention to angels in Christ-communities (2 Corinthians 11:13-14; Colossians 2:18).

We should also clarify that the words "form," "likeness," and "appearance" do not necessarily shade toward simple similarity short of equality. There was an early school of thought known as Docetism that claimed Christ merely seemed to be a human being, looked like a human being, but was not really human because God would never lower God's self to flesh and blood. In this view, Jesus Christ masqueraded in a human costume for a brief earthly performance. But make no mistake: Paul roundly rejected this idea. Jesus Christ was no play-actor in a human drama. Just as he was in the full "form of God," he was also in the full "form" of humanity, a full-fledged, flesh-and-blood person.

If that's not enough to boggle the mind, Christ was a particular human being, "taking the form of a slave" (Philippians 2:7). It's hard to imagine any status more opposite from the exalted God than an enslaved person. Slavery was widespread in Roman society, with slaves making up a significant portion of the population. Slaves served in various capacities, from brutal forced labor in mines to more congenial duty in household management. But at whatever level of employment, slaves were not free persons; they remained subject to the wills and whims of human lords and masters, from Caesar to male household heads.

Things get tricky, then, when Paul says that the God-form Christ became a human-form slave. Though Jesus was no elite nobleman, he was never a literal slave. He came from a lowly working-class Jewish family in the backwater hamlet of Nazareth. But he was still legally a freedman, though subject to Roman colonial rule, like all Jews at the time. In this case, "form of a slave" must be limited to similarity, not equality. Christ was like a slave in the more usual sense of "like." Even so, the slave simile packs a wallop!

Being compared to a slave in the company of slaves is something no self-respecting Roman citizen would tolerate for a second. Yet that's precisely the point the hymn underscores. God-in-Christ comes to earth in full identification with all human beings, including the least and lowliest slaves.

From preexistent equality with God to earthly solidarity with human slaves: By all appearances, that would suggest a colossal demotion for Christ or total evacuation of his high position. Or in the language of the hymn, an utter emptying of his former glory, a self-emptying, no less, that Christ willingly chose (2:8). Such a striking act of humility is commonly interpreted as a sign of Christ's amazing grace and love. Look at all Christ gave up coming to earth to save us broken human beings. Thanks be to Christ. Amen. But that's not the last word on the subject.

Consider more closely what Christ emptied himself of and why. "Emptying" may evoke images of pouring out a container's contents and replacing it with another substance. By this logic, we might think Christ decanted his divine essence and refilled his "form" with human nature—a total makeover or shape-shift. But this pushes the image too far for Paul's theology. While Christ clearly limited his divine powers and privileges during his time on earth—as a human being, he needed to eat, drink, and rest and was subject to suffering and death—he did not divest himself of his special identity and intimate relationship with God the Father and the Spirit (1:2, 19).

In some sense, the divine and human "forms" completely merged in Jesus Christ, the God-Hu/man. Paul would be the first to stress that the mechanics of this merger are a profound mystery (see Romans 16:25-27; Colossians 2:2-3; 1 Timothy 3:16). It can't be isolated or reproduced in a biology lab. But the world is full of unexplained mysteries, not least regarding the mystery of life itself. By living with and into these mysteries—with and in Christ, to repeat Paul's core conviction—we experience richer and fuller lives.

Accepting the mystery of Christ's incarnation, however, raises the question of Christ's motivation in this process. Remember, Christ chose his earthly, human mission; he was not coerced by God. So what drove his dramatic transformation and "career change"? A scholar-friend of mine, David Fredrickson from Luther Seminary in St. Paul, Minnesota, offers a compelling answer. He highlights "self-emptying" language and imagery in Greek and Latin poetry associated with lovers' passionate longing for one another, especially during times of absence. Absence doesn't merely make the heart grow fonder. Absence aches and agitates, longs and liquefies, making the heart melt, drain, bleed, pour out—empty! Applied to Christ, this suggests we should not primarily see his self-emptying into human life as condescension or humiliation but rather as the passion to be with his beloved people as intimately as possible in their sufferings as well as their joys.

Christ did not so much lower himself to become human as fulfill his own longing for deep union with humanity. His goal was less to come down and clean up the mess people had made than to be with them as one of them—amid the mess. And if that seems like a shameful thing for God's Son to do, then so be it. Lovers are unabashed, shameless (as Billy Joel's great song "Shameless" attests). Lovers are all in for their beloveds, regardless of what anyone else thinks.

Christ's Cross-Execution

Even more dramatic than Christ's transition from preexistence to self-emptying is his excruciating "death—even death on a cross" (Philippians 2:8)—a forced, pierced, public emptying of lifeblood. Again, this is an extraordinary fate for God in any "form." The notion of the Crucified God, as the eminent theologian Jürgen Moltmann titled his monumental book,[1] is utterly flabbergasting, radical in the extreme, even "scandalous" and "foolish" (1 Corinthians 1:18-25).

Only slightly less unthinkable would be Christ's bloody execution if he were an angelic being in human camouflage, especially given his retort to his arrestors in Matthew 26:53: "Do you think that I cannot appeal to my Father, and he will at once send me more than twelve legions of angels?" In the Bible, angels are part of God's rescue squad, who occasionally kill captors and threateners of God's children, but again, angels themselves do not die, as Jesus did. And more to the point, Christ commanded no angelic SWAT team and issued no kill orders to save himself.

There are biblical examples of righteous people who suffer for their faithful commitment to God, even unto death as martyrs (Isaiah 53; 2 Maccabees 6:18–7:42). But whatever encouragement they might provide fellow sufferers, they were not held up as models of God's saving Son or Messiah via crucifixion. A crucified God or crucified Messiah is unprecedented and virtually inconceivable.

Things get even crazier if you bring in politics. The cross was Caesar's trump card, the chief weapon of lethal force against threats to the Roman Empire, real or imagined. The cross was for treacherous rebels, violent criminals, and captured enemies, as defined by the state. For his part, Jesus promoted and embodied the supreme rule (kingdom) of God, but he never called for the overthrow of the Roman government by violent means. His execution was an unconscionable miscarriage of justice.

And yet it happened. God let it happen. Christ let it happen. And believers in God and Christ celebrate it in song, like the Philippians hymn and other cherished songs through the ages, such as "When I Survey the Wondrous Cross" and "The Old Rugged Cross." The cross became the central sign of saving faith in Christian art and architecture, to say nothing of cross-shaped jewelry and body tattoos in our day. Crosses are sacred, even "cool," in Christian circles, so much so that we can easily forget how shocking and horrific they were in Paul's time.

Elsewhere, Paul unpacks the significance of Christ's crucifixion in God's plan of salvation (Romans 5:6-21; 1 Corinthians 1:17-31; Galatians 3:10-14). But not in Philippians. Here, Paul simply announces the bare fact of Christ's death on a cross in all its gobsmacking wonder (awe) and horror (awfulness). "Behold the man!" as the Roman governor, Pilate, infamously said of Jesus before delivering him to be crucified (John 19:5). The Philippians hymn summons us to pause and "behold the man" Jesus on the cross.

And as we behold the crucified Christ, we must not ignore one brief clarifying point Paul makes in the hymn: "He... became obedient to the point of death— / even death on a cross" (Philippians 2:8). Christ didn't simply accept his cross fate; he obeyed an order to take up the cross and die. Whose order, pray tell? Paul doesn't say, but he's certainly not implying that Christ obeyed Pilate's kill order. In God's eye and Paul's, Pilate and his boss Caesar had no legitimate authority over God's Son. Apart from his earthly parents during his youth (Luke 2:51-52), the only one Jesus was obligated to obey was his divine Father.

But that creates for me an unbearable cross crisis. I'm not alone in this. Are we supposed to accept that the loving God commanded his beloved Son to submit himself to crucifixion? That smacks of child sacrifice. It's impossible for me as a parent and grandparent, even with all my shortcomings, to conceive of sending my innocent children and grandchildren to their deaths for any reason by any means, least of all torturous execution. And I would hope they would defiantly reject any such order. Of course, I may simply be revealing my immaturity, sentimentality, and unwillingness to obey God's will at all costs. I also struggle with Abraham's willingness in Genesis 22 to sacrifice his son Isaac at God's behest, to say nothing of Isaac's blithe submission, though thankfully, in this case, God stays Abraham's slaying hand at the last moment.

The best I can do with these "obedience to death" dilemmas is to fall back on unfathomable mystery and ineffable love. I'm fortunate enough in my life to have known, felt, and shared love in some measure, but I don't pretend to grasp the depths of eternal love flowing between God and Christ or how faithful obedience might figure into that bond. I know Jesus sought to do his Father's will. But I also have an inkling that the infinite love between the coequal God and Christ is more mutual than hierarchical, perfectly blending give and take, trust and obedience.

I put a lot of stock in the emotional Gospel story (though Paul never mentions it) where Jesus struggles with God's will on the eve of his crucifixion, fervently pleading with his divine Abba to keep him from the cross, "if it were [at all] possible" (Mark 14:35-36; cf. 14:32-36; Matthew 26:36-39; Luke 22:39-44). I suggest that Jesus's famous conclusion, "Yet not my will but yours be done" (Mark 14:36, NCB), doesn't tie a neat bow around the situation, as if to aver, "Okay, that's settled then. Aye, aye, Father. Onward march to the cross!" Rather, it reflects an intense, intimate wrestling of wills (desires, aims, interests) within the melded loving heart of God the Father and God the Son. In some profound sense beyond my understanding, God the Father, whose essence is love, died with God the Son—not by dying on the cross himself, but through the immeasurable love binding Father and Son together. For the sake of a broken world, the crucified Christ revealed the brokenhearted love of God.

Christ's High Exaltation

If you're familiar with Christ's story, you naturally expect Christ's crucifixion to be overcome by resurrection. I frequently use the hyphenated form, crucifixion-resurrection, to reflect this close connection. In Paul's first Philippians reference, however, to Christ's crucifixion (2:8), he doesn't directly move to Christ's resurrection. He postpones mentioning "the power of [Christ's] resurrection" until 3:10. So maybe Paul didn't write the hymn lyrics in 2:6-11 after all, though if not, it's surprising he didn't add a line about resurrection.

Perhaps I'm making too big a deal out of this omission, particularly since the hymn swiftly shifts from the "cross" reference to the rousing finale of Christ's high exaltation (2:9). Doesn't exaltation assume resurrection? How else might a crucified victim be "exalted"? Well, in fact, martyrs by any mode of execution have been highly honored posthumously, apart from prospects of resurrection.

Concerning the Philippians hymn, I don't think it suggests Christ's death as martyrdom, and I do think it implies Christ's resurrection in his exaltation. Yet its moving directly from Christ's crucifixion to exaltation tightly fuses Christ's cross and crown, so to speak, transforming his mock crown of thorns into a true mark of glory. In other words, Jesus is glorified on the cross before he gets off it and is raised up to new life. Resurrection certifies Christ's exaltation, but it doesn't initiate it. To use a marvelous play on words from John's Gospel, Jesus was *lifted up* on the cross both in the physical sense of hoisted on a wooden crossbeam and in the metaphorical sense of honored in exaltation (John 3:14-15; 8:28; 12:32-33). The glory of the cross is not masochistic. It's not good or fun to suffer! But it is mystery and metaphor, paradox and parable, which Jesus specialized in with statements like, "Those who want to save their life will lose it" (Mark 8:35), and "Whoever wants to be first must be last of all and servant of all" (Mark 9:35). The cross in itself marks the climax of Christ's stupendous self-emptying love, draining his very lifeblood for all people, including the lowliest of slaves and criminals—those most likely to suffer crucifixion.

Although Christ's crucifixion begins his exaltation by God, it doesn't end it, not by a long shot. The cross sparks a cosmic renewal of all creation stamped with the name of Jesus Christ,

> *so that at the name given to Jesus*
> *every knee should bend,*
> *in heaven and on earth and under the earth,*
> *and every tongue should confess*
> *that Jesus Christ is Lord,*
> *to the glory of God the Father.*
> (*Philippians 2:10-11*)

The whole universe—celestial (heaven), terrestrial (earth), and subterranean (under the earth)—falls under the lordship of the cocreating God and Christ. Notice the explicit merging of heaven and earth, emphasizing the entirety of earth, above and below ground. All creatures great and small, from archangels, earthly kings, and mighty beasts to the lowest organisms deep in soils and swamps, will acknowledge Jesus Christ as Lord.

With this soaring crescendo, we might be inclined to sing Philippians 2:6-11 as a thunderous battle hymn, signaling the divine triumphal counterblast against an evil world that conspired to crucify Christ. But such a militant strain clashes with Jesus's radical call to love and forgive enemies (Luke 6:27-36; 23:34-43; cf. Romans 12:14-21). Moreover, not everyone spurns Christ's outreaching love, as Paul and his Philippian siblings in Christ, including some members of "the emperor's household" (Philippians 4:21-22), attest.

And to take seriously the "under the earth" sphere, while some diabolical "underworld" agents sought to do away with Christ, many poor, weak sufferers under the thumb of oppressive strongmen welcomed Christ's uplifting ministry of compassion (1 Corinthians 1:26-31).

Further, what about the billions of creepy-crawly creatures made by God (Genesis 1:24-26) that literally live or burrow underground? Why must they be brought to their knees to honor Christ?

I know this literalism pushes the limits of poetic language, but please indulge a quirky thought experiment that helps me appreciate the mind-blowing scope of the Philippians hymn. Since "every knee" will bend before Christ, imagine all one thousand knees of all millipedes kneeling at Christ's feet. I have no idea if these arthropods have anatomical knees, and Google AI tells me their appendages vary, though one millipede has been found with 1,306 legs (pity the poor lab assistant who counted them). But that's beside the point, which is that the self-emptying, crucified, exalted Christ seeks to restore all creation and creatures, however tiny and seemingly trivial, under the canopy of his infinite outpouring love. I think Saint Francis of Assisi and Albert Schweitzer, to name two famous lovers of all living things, would be happy with my millipede example.

The point is not how many kneecaps Christ can bust and voices he can command to praise him. That's what spiteful strongmen aspire to do, not the Lord of life and love. The point is bowing knees together in mutual submission and raising voices together in mutual support—with and in Christ. God, Christ, the universe, and the environment interlink in a dynamic partnership. If you're keeping score of academic "-ologies," that's theology, Christology, cosmology, and ecology working together for the common good (Romans 8:18-39; Philippians 1:5-6; 2:12-13).

The Exemplary Life Story of Christ

Having tracked the stages of Christ's model life story, we now explore how Paul applies this in Philippians to four characters: (1) the Philippian congregation (Philippians 2:1-4, 12-18), (2) Paul himself (2:17-18; 3:17-4:1), (3) Timothy (2:19-24), and (4) Epaphroditus (2:25-30).

The Philippian Congregation

The "you" in 2:5 Paul exhorts to cultivate Christ's mindset and lifestyle is plural, encompassing the whole group of believers, not just the leaders. Paul reinforces this inclusive responsibility in the preceding verse, when he urges, "Let each of you look not to your own interests but to the interests of others" (2:4). This resonates with Christ's consideration of all people's interests, especially those of the poorest and lowliest, at the expense of his powerful position, which he refused to exploit (2:6-7).

Likewise, in 2:1-3, Paul calls the Philippian assembly to treat one another with consoling "love" and "tender affection," committed to "do nothing from selfish ambition and empty conceit, but in humility regard others as better than yourselves." The term politely rendered "tender affection" (*splanchna*), also used to describe Christ's feelings in 1:8, carries a stronger, cruder sense of gut-level compassion; the term literally means "bowels"! Such stirring sympathy "moved" Jesus to aid a desperate widow who had just lost her only son (Luke 7:11-17; cf. 10:33-37; 15:20-24). And the references to "empty conceit" and "humility" in Philippians 2:3 echo the ensuing hymn's emphasis on Christ's emptying and humbling himself in passionate outpouring love toward all humanity (2:7-8).

Paul

As a true servant-pastor, Paul never asks congregants to do anything he's not already modeled and aims to keep doing. Shortly after citing the Christ hymn, Paul opens his heart to "my beloved" ones (2:12), professing, "Even if I am being poured out as libation over the sacrifice and service of your faith, I rejoice" (2:17). A little later he urges his "brothers and sisters" to "join in imitating me and observe those who live according to the example you have in us" (3:17). In this context, "imitation" reflects a genuine desire to follow someone's admirable way of life, not to mock them with cheap impersonation (think imitation jewelry).

Of course, Paul only calls the Philippians to imitate him as he imitates Christ (cf. 1 Corinthians 4:16; 11:1), especially the crucified Christ featured in the hymn. Paul embraces the way of the cross in contrast to "enemies of the cross of Christ" (Philippians 3:18). His "being poured out" for the sake of his Philippian family in Christ, "whom I love and long for" (4:1; cf. 1:8), mirrors Christ's self-emptying to melt into and meld with his dear human loved ones, even unto death.

There's a long-standing tradition of imitating Christ. The fifteenth-century devotional book *The Imitation of Christ* by Thomas à Kempis remains a religious classic.[2] We might imagine Philippians as a chain letter of imitative love running from God → Christ → Paul → the Philippian believers or, better, as a dynamic, circulating network of divine-human longing and love embodied in the passionate God-Hu/man Jesus Christ.

And let's not forget Paul's drumbeat of mutual joy in this process. Notice his assessment of sacrificial outpouring for his friends as a source of co-rejoicing: "I rejoice together with all of you; in the same way also you should rejoice and rejoice together with me" (2:17-18). Why is carrying the cross of Christ not a miserable, trudging, grudging duty? Because it is carried together with Christ and one another in a buoyant Spirit of sympathetic love (see 2:1-2).

Timothy, Paul's "Son"

Though Paul is not lacking in self-confidence and ego-strength, he's no narcissist or egomaniac. While boldly proclaiming himself a Christlike exemplar, he doesn't hog the spotlight or hail himself as Christ's supreme representative. Paul participates in living the Christ-centered life with "all the saints in Christ Jesus" (1:1) collectively and with certain co-ministers in particular.

One of Paul's closest associates is a younger man named Timothy. According to Acts, Timothy was of mixed Jewish (mother) and Greek (father) parentage. Paul recruited Timothy as a promising "disciple" to join his missionary venture into Macedonia, which began with proclaiming the gospel to Lydia and her household in Philippi (Acts 16:1-15). So Timothy was well-known to the Philippian congregation, which explains why Paul mentions him at the start of the letter (Philippians 1:1) and now proposes to send him to help the community in Paul's stead (2:23).

One reason Paul trusts Timothy is their shared "family" history, spiritually and vocationally: "Timothy's worth you know, how like a son with a father he has served with me in the work of the gospel" (2:22). Timothy was no ordinary apprentice Paul took on but more like an adopted son working side by side in the family gospel business. The arrangement was less patriarchal than cooperative. Timothy "has served with me," Paul insists.

More than that, this "served" term (*douleuō*) connotes joint slave service, linking back both to the opening designation of Paul and Timothy as "servants/slaves [*douloi*] of Christ Jesus" (1:1) and to the hymn's characterization of Christ's human slave "form" (*morphēn doulou* [2:7]). Again, Paul and Timothy follow Christ's example of sympathizing with marginalized "others" commonly regarded as deplorable and expendable.

In Paul's view, Timothy excels with Paul in this self-giving, other-serving imitation of Christ: "I have no one so like myself who will be genuinely concerned for your welfare. All of them are seeking their own interests, not those of Jesus Christ" (2:20-21). Self-seekers would include rival preachers mentioned in 1:14-17 who sought to make hay while Paul was in prison. In contrast, by seeking others' interests above his own, Timothy follows Paul's example and counsel (see 2:3-4, 17).

And note well that Paul's commendation of Timothy as "no one so like myself" focuses on Timothy's moral character and social concern

(2:20), not on his personal loyalty to Paul. In other words, Paul is not obsessed with image-building by tallying sycophantic "likes" but rather motivated to prompt Christ-likeness in loving service to others.

Epaphroditus, Paul's "Brother"

We've already met Epaphroditus as the Philippians' messenger to Paul in prison, bearing their care package (4:18), offering personal assistance, and probably carrying this letter back to his home church (2:28). Yet Epaphroditus is no mere errand boy or nominal servant but rather a beloved member of the Philippian fellowship and valued partner with Paul in "the work of Christ" (2:30).

Paul first names Epaphroditus, followed by five personal descriptors: "my [1] brother and [2] coworker and [3] fellow soldier, your [4] messenger and [5] minister to my need" (2:25). That's quite a list ranging across familial, ministerial, and military spheres of service. Of course, there was no literal sword-bearing Christian militia in Paul's day (we're centuries away from the Crusades). But the struggles Paul references with rivals, opposers, and "enemies of the cross" could feel like battles. (I've been in a few church conferences that felt like a fight to the death, even over trivial matters. Sigh.)

The last two labels Paul pins on Epaphroditus are particularly intriguing. First, "messenger" is a good rendering of *apostolos*, literally "sent one" (the verb *apostellō* means "send"), befitting the fact that Epaphroditus is sent back and forth between the Philippians and Paul. But Paul could have easily used other "messenger" terms. Instead, he chooses the one term he most often uses to certify his own calling as Christ's apostle, one sent directly by Christ. Yet while Paul staunchly defends his apostolic authority against detractors (1 Corinthians 15:3-11; Galatians 1:1, 11-17; 2:6-9), he does not jealously restrict the "apostle" title to himself or to one of Jesus's original twelve apostles. For example, he's happy to include Andronicus and Junia, likely a married couple, among the "prominent" ranks of "apostles" (Romans 16:7)—and Epaphroditus too. In the inclusive community of Christ, to be sent by a local group of believers or by an apostle like Paul is to be sent by Christ as a co-apostle, a messenger-partner of Christ among a mutual cadre of sent-ones.

Second, the "minister" term (*leitourgos*) identifying Epaphroditus connotes a "social worker," more literally, a "worker for the people/laity." Again, this title is less a marker of superior office than of supportive service. Paul rarely uses this word, but when he does, it applies to offerings of both material gifts (Romans 15:16; 2 Corinthians 9:12) and personal selves for others' sake. It's in this latter sense that Paul characterizes his own work in Philippians 2:17, which I now requote to highlight its "liturgical" imagery: "But even if I am being poured out as a libation over the sacrifice and the service (*leitourgia*) of your faith, I rejoice, and I rejoice together with all of you." Paul thus bolsters his generous, joyous bond of love with Epaphroditus and fellow Philippians. As Epaphroditus gladly delivers the Philippians' gracious aid to Paul, he's happily prepared to drain his last ounce of life for them.

And as a true co-minister with Paul, Epaphroditus also puts his life on the line. Though sparing with details, Paul shares that Epaphroditus "nearly died" from some illness during his mission to help Paul, thereby triggering much anxious concern on Paul's part for his dear friend. Likewise, Epaphroditus was beside himself, not for his own health but out of deep "longing" to see his beloved church family and ease their distress over his welfare (2:26-28). A truly moving picture of mutual compassion: Epaphroditus "came close to death for the work of Christ, risking his life to make up for those services [*leitourgias*] you could not give me" (2:30).

Moreover, the prospect of Epaphroditus's "death for the work of Christ" aligns with Christ's own slave-empathizing, self-emptying death for his longed-for loved ones (Philippians 2:7-8). Having a common slave name, Epaphroditus may have been an actual slave. The fact that some Christians owned slaves in Paul's day is one of those inconvenient truths we can't escape.

In another prison letter, Paul writes to a house church leader named Philemon about a slave Philemon owned named Onesimus, meaning "useful." Paul had recently met Onesimus and become his "father" in Christ (Philemon 10). Paul sends Onesimus back to Philemon with the letter, urging Philemon to receive Onesimus back "no longer as a slave but more than a slave, a beloved brother—especially to me but how much more to you, both in the flesh and in the Lord" (Philemon 16). This is the closest we get to an emancipation proclamation from Paul. But the matter is left unresolved. The same is true of Epaphroditus; we can't be certain of his legal status. But whether he was a freedman or an enslaved person, Paul demonstrates the same fervent family feeling for him as he does for Onesimus. Paul treats them both as equals.

CHAPTER 5

The Stretch Toward Christ

Key Passage
Philippians 3:1-16

American sprinter Noah Lyles won the 100-meter gold medal at the 2024 Paris Olympics by the minuscule margin of four-thousandths (.004) of a second. He nosed out the second-place runner by a head stretch at the finish line. Four days later, Lyles took the bronze medal in the 200-meter race, but arguably this was more impressive than the shorter dash. Now he stretched every fiber of his body for the entire race, pressing through the draining effects of a COVID-19 infection. Understandably, after crossing the finish line, Lyles collapsed with exhaustion—but also with a deep sense of satisfaction.

Elite athletes don't just stretch to loosen their muscles before and after performances. Their whole career is one passionate, rigorous stretch to reach the goal line.

In Philippians 3:1-16, Paul reflects on his life as a race he's running, not as occasional sprints but as an extended marathon. It was common in Paul's day to imagine life as a path or course one traverses, like a long walk, hike, or trek. The notion of a life-race also evokes a moving picture, but one that's more energetic and goal-directed, more straining and outstretching. We're familiar with the negative image of an exhausting "rat race" through a frustrating maze or around a caged wheel. But some people love to run to get ahead financially or get in better physical shape. They love the thrill of the chase.

Paul views his life-race in positive, though not exactly thrilling, terms, and he cares little about earthly prizes. Here's his running philosophy in a nutshell: "I press on to lay hold of that [goal] for which Christ has laid hold of me. . . . [F]orgetting what lies behind and straining forward to what lies ahead, I press toward the goal, toward the prize of the heavenly call of God in Christ Jesus" (3:12-14). There's much to unpack here. But from the start, we should remember Paul's Christ-centered life mission that runs throughout Philippians. As Olympic track stars run for their countries' pride and honor, Paul runs for Christ's glory and "gain" (3:7-8).

The Race Is On

We've already noted Paul's likening his shared ministry with his Philippian Christ-partners to athletic teamwork, "striving side by side [*synathlountes*]" like fellow athletes "for the faith of the gospel" (1:27). A few verses later, he uses a term for their common "struggle" (*agōn*) that can also mean "contest" or competitive "race" (1:30). Toward the end of the letter, Paul uses more sports language to commend Euodia and Syntyche, a pair of women ministerial leaders, "for they have struggled beside [*synathlēsan*] me" like valued teammates "in the work of the gospel" (4:2-3). Paul is no solo flyer. He strives to be both a team player and a player-coach.

More directly characterizing his partnership with the Philippians as a running operation, Paul urges his beloved associates to follow his lead "so that I can boast on the day of Christ that I did not run in vain or labor in vain" (2:16; cf. Galatians 2:2). Paul "boasts" tongue in cheek to mock his self-promoting rivals and stress what's really worth boasting about. For example, "I will boast all the more gladly of my weaknesses, so that the power of Christ may dwell in me" (2 Corinthians 12:9;

see 12:1-10; 1 Corinthians 1:31–2:5; 3:18-23). In Philippians 2:16, Paul hopes to "boast on the day of Christ"—that is, the time of Christ's ultimate reconciliation of the world (see 2:9-11)—that his life's work genuinely advanced Christ's mission. Not that Paul needs to impress Christ or pile up credits to earn Christ's favor. The judgment of Christ trades on love, grace, mercy, and forgiveness, not on plea deals and pompous displays. But Paul wants his running for and toward Christ to count for something good and noble, not "vain" and vacuous.

A key cross-reference to Paul's "running" philosophy appears in 1 Corinthians 9 against the backdrop of the popular Olympic-style Isthmian Games held biennially in Corinth:

> *Do you not know that in a race the runners all compete, but only one receives the prize? Run in such a way that you [all] may win it. Athletes exercise self-control in all things; they do it to receive a perishable wreath, but we an imperishable one. So I do not run aimlessly, nor do I box as though beating the air, but I punish my body and enslave it, so that after proclaiming to others I myself should not be disqualified.*
>
> *(1 Corinthians 9:24-27)*

A quick read might suggest Paul pushes a "winning only" agenda. "Only one [runner] receives the prize," so be in it to win it. Being "number one" is all that matters; everyone else is a loser. Much of the American sports scene is driven by this attitude, and male preachers (and politicians) have a penchant for using heroic sports illustrations. I might have used one or two (or twenty) in sermons through the years. Paul takes a nuanced approach, both comparing and contrasting Christlike living and competing.

On the comparative side, Paul values discipline and focus. Dedicated contestants don't just show up on the day of the big race or game. "Athletes exercise self-control in all things" (9:25). Winning depends on rigorous preparation, training, and strategizing before the event. And during the event, they don't run around "aimlessly" or flail their arms willy-nilly (Paul adds a boxing image). Runners must remain laser-focused on the finish line, and boxers must target their opponents' weak spots. As we will see in Philippians 3, Paul is clear-eyed about the optimal means and ends of running like and toward Christ.

On the contrastive side, Paul makes two critical distinctions in 1 Corinthians 9. First, a numerical distinction. He introduces the race-running metaphor in individual terms: "Do you not know that in a race the runners all compete, but only one receives the [top] prize?" (9:24). Of course, we know. That's the way races work. That's why we developed photo-finish technology. But Paul describes the race run by Christ-followers as a communal affair: "Run in such a way that you [all, plural] may win it" (9:24). Paul is not promoting a soft policy that everybody gets a "participation trophy" for showing up. The "way" each one runs the Christ-race matters, bringing us back to the virtues of discipline and determination. So run as if the honor of the whole Christ-community depends on you individually. But also know you can only hope to go the distance with the support and strength of Christ and all your teammates. Think relay race.

Paul again stresses his personal commitment to the Christ-led race. As far as we know, Paul was no great physical athlete; his short bowlegs, per the one body profile we have from an apocryphal text (see chapter 1), would not a speedster make! And what we know of his former persecution of Christ-followers scarcely commends him as a Christlike pacesetter. Moreover, even after his dramatic transformation by Christ, Paul does not rest on his apostolic laurels but rather sets out to prove his mettle as a dedicated "runner," "so that after proclaiming [the gospel] to others I myself should not be disqualified" from the race (9:26-27). Any prize he wins, he owes to Christ and shares with the whole Christ-squad.

Second, Paul makes a sharp distinction in prize value. World-class Greco-Roman athletes competed for head wreaths fashioned from leaves and branches of the bay laurel tree, hence our honorific terms "laurel" and "laureate." Wild celery could also serve in a pinch. Pretty crowns for as long as they last, which is not very long! Wilting leaves and crumbling branches do not project strength and stamina. They are, as Paul says, "perishable" items, whereas runners on Team Christ press toward "imperishable" goals of eternal value (9:25; cf. Philippians 3:10-14). To update the prize, gold medals are more durable and valuable than leafy laurels, but they're still subject to tarnish, corrosion, and theft.

Running from Rubbish Toward Christ

Successful runners streamline their bodies and clothing to reduce the drag on their progress. Modern track stars sport sleek, muscular bodies in scanty wind-resistant attire. Ancient Greek runners went even scantier, competing in the nude: buff athletes in the buff.

My first track-and-field feat in elementary school was a timed 50-yard dash. Coach Whisenant was not pleased because I'd run in my normal, hard, clunky school shoes. This was before every kid owned multiple designer sneakers. Coach yelled at me to ditch my shoes and run again. Tenderfoot though I was, I ran the dash again barefoot and cut almost a full second off my time. I felt like The Flash! I eventually got one pair of brand-name gym shoes in high school.

In coaching the Christ-focused race of life, New Testament writers urge believers to run as free and loose as possible from inhibiting baggage. The author of Hebrews exhorts, "Lay aside every weight and the sin that clings so closely, and...run with perseverance the race that [Jesus] set before us" (12:1-2). In Philippians, Paul speaks hyperbolically and paradoxically of "los[ing] all things...in order that I may gain [win] Christ...forgetting what lies behind" (3:8, 13). Sounds like leaving it all behind for Christ, not just sin but all former relations and possessions, as Jesus called his disciples to do (Mark 1:16-20; 8:34-35; 10:21-31).

Upping the ante with an unforgettable image, in Philippians 3:8 Paul discounts everything in his life before knowing Christ as so much "rubbish," "sewer trash" (CEB), "garbage" (NIV), or "dung" (KJV). Curiously, one of the first phrases my young granddaughter repeatedly said was "yucky garbage" (I couldn't help laughing every time). That would work fine here too. In race terms, Paul effectively says, "If you want to run rightly toward Christ, you've got to clear out the yucky garbage strewn on the track from your old life, lest it trip you up." And that includes more than the obviously bad, sinful stuff.

Paul had a lot going for him in his "before Christ" career, with impressive qualifications that carried over into his "after Christ" ministry. In modern high-level competitions, runners must succeed in qualifying heats to participate in the final contest. Paul has good "reason for confidence" (Philippians 3:4) in securing a prime lane for the medal race—five reasons, as we will see, to "boast" and place himself ahead of others (3:3-6). But this is precisely what he refuses to do. Far from crowing about his achievements, Paul consigns them to the rubbish pile "because of the surpassing value of knowing Jesus my Lord" (3:8). His relationship with Christ is all that matters. Everything else is dead weight.

Beyond clarifying Paul's Christ-consumed running strategy, his Christlike self-emptying (cf. 2:7) throws the race wide open to all Christ-adherents, regardless of social status, economic worth, or other identity markers. The race toward Christ is a race of grace "so that no one may boast" (Ephesians 2:8-9). As the imprisoned Paul and beleaguered Philippians struggle together as low-ranking runners in society, they find mutual strength and encouragement in Christ to press on with joy and hope in the race that truly counts (Philippians 3:12-14).

To help us appreciate the wide, level track Christ has opened, it's useful to provide a short sketch of Paul's five credentials that he came to see as unnecessary for participating in Team Christ's grace-fueled race. Unfortunately, societies and communities, including faith communities, still use these standards to divide and exclude people.

Ethnic Identity

Paul has a solid pedigree as a native member of God's chosen people: "circumcised on the eighth day, a member of the people of Israel, of the tribe of Benjamin, a Hebrew born of Hebrews" (3:5). (Paul's Jewish name was Saul, in honor of Israel's first king, a descendant of Benjamin.) Paul ticks all the qualifying boxes. Paul runs his life-race in the footsteps of famed faithful forerunners like Abraham, Moses, and ultimately Jesus, comprising a "great cloud of witnesses" setting the pace and cheering on Paul and fellow runners (Hebrews 12:1-2).

But God's love and care for Israel are not exclusive. From the start, God's elective purpose has been to bless "all the families of the earth" through Abraham's people (Genesis 12:1-3). While Christ particularly called Paul to be God's "apostle to the gentiles [*ethnōn*]" (Romans 1:5; 11:13; Galatians 2:8), Paul never renounces his Jewish heritage. How could he, since he proclaims the Jew Jesus as God's anointed Messiah? But ancestry does not determine the Christ-race, whether the metaphorical athletic race or the biological genetic race. Neither Jewish, Greek, Roman, nor any other ethnic status gives you a leg up in this event.

Gender Role

All the biblical talk about circumcision can seem very strange to modern readers, but historically, it represented a critical badge of Jewish identity, marking the covenantal bond between God and Israel (Genesis 17). But, of course, it's an exclusively male mark, incised on baby boys' sexual organs at eight days of age, as happened with infant Paul (or later for gentile converts).

So what did this mean for Israel's women? They were certainly not excluded from the community. Women were obviously essential to carrying on the covenant line. But like most women in Mediterranean antiquity, Jewish women were generally regarded as subordinate to men's authority. Paul was no first-century feminist (there were none then). Yet, as previously noted, Paul respected women church leaders like Euodia and Syntyche (and Lydia) as sister "athletic" participants and coaches (Philippians 4:2-3).

Paul does not dismiss circumcision as a significant Jewish rite, but he discounts it as a prerequisite for entering God's realm. He simply resists imposing it on non-Jews who believe in Christ. He tends to use strong language in denouncing Jewish Christ-confessors who insist that gentiles' salvation depends not only on faith in Christ but also on faithfulness to Jewish law (Torah), starting with circumcision. In Philippians, he calls these circumcision advocates "dogs" (predatory curs) and "evil workers . . . who mutilate the flesh" (3:2). This is slightly better, though not much, than wishing in Galatians 5:11-12 that circumcisers' knives would slip and they would "castrate themselves"! Eesh.

In the predominantly gentile fellowship in Philippi, the circumcision issue seems to be a potential threat they should "beware" (Philippians 3:2) more than an active problem. But in any case, no women or uncircumcised gentile believers in Christ need fear missing the "cut" as qualified runners. The track and field is gender and ethnic inclusive.

Party Affiliation

Before his transformation by Christ, Paul was a law-loving Pharisee (3:5). Acts identifies him as "a son of Pharisees" (Acts 23:6). It's a family tradition, a good one. Pharisees were respected scholars and teachers of Torah. In Jesus's case, despite sharp disagreements with the Pharisees over various issues, he admired their commitment to studying the

Scriptures and applying them to everyday life. And not only Paul but other Pharisees, too, became Christ-adherents (15:5).

First-century Pharisees were not exactly an official religious or political group (no ID cards or secret handshakes), but they resembled what we call a religious denomination and a political party. Religion and politics were closely entwined in Paul's world. Again, however, Coach Paul implies, "Support your denomination or party all you want. Cheer on your favorite runners. Make as many banners as you want, but don't use these as barriers to ban others. The Christ racecourse is wide open."

Religious Dedication

Paul possessed intense religious "zeal" (Philippians 3:6). This is another positive quality—mostly. Most pastors would welcome more passion for God in their congregations. Nothing kills a church's effectiveness faster than "lukewarm" mediocrity (Revelation 3:14-22). Zeal is a great energizer, provided it's wisely managed. In a marathon, you can't go full bore without burning out. You must run smart with the right mentality—the mind of Christ—in Paul's view (Philippians 2:5). Elsewhere, Paul cautions against those who "have a zeal for God . . . not based on knowledge" (Romans 10:2). It's all heat with little light.

Paul knows what he's talking about. It's the least attractive element of his past. Before his life-changing encounter with Christ, Paul became so zealously obsessed with his convictions that he felt duty-bound not simply to promote his belief system but to eliminate the upstart Jesus sect. Hence, he became a militant "persecutor of the church" (Philippians 3:6; cf. 1 Corinthians 15:9; Galatians 1:13-14). Note well: This was not normal Pharisee behavior. This was radical extremism based on narrow knowledge, which can ensnare even the most devout people. All religions, sadly, have their hyperzealots who will elbow, trip, and bowl over their competitors and do anything to control the racetrack. Such is not the mindset of the servant Christ.

Conduct Record

Throughout his life, Paul diligently sought to play by the rules and obey God's commandments. In Galatians 1:14, he says he "advanced in Judaism beyond many among my people of the same age," and in Philippians 3:6, he claims to be "blameless" regarding "righteousness under the [Jewish] law," that is, scrupulously compliant with Torah. No blots on Paul's record challenge his fitness for God's team.

But totally spotless? Hardly. The Christ-serving Paul would judge his former self-image as smugly self-righteous. We'll explore Paul's more enlightened view of righteousness in the next section; for now, notwithstanding his perfectionist pretenses, we should appreciate that Paul had long strived to be a good person and high achiever: the proverbial model citizen, straight-A student, big man on campus—and religious track star!

There's nothing inherently wrong with Paul's pedigree and pursuits (minus the violence). "Be all you can be" (U.S. Army slogan), but not at others' expense or to pump up one's sense of superiority. Being as virtuous as one can be is good, but that doesn't make you better than anyone else or more qualified to run Christ's race. It's a grace race, remember, for all who stumble and stagger, which is all of us (Romans 3:9-10, 23). Recall Paul's charge right before the Philippians hymn, "Do nothing from selfish ambition or empty conceit, but in humility regard others as better than yourselves" (2:3).

Flourishing living in Christ commends solidarity and compassion over singularity and competition. It allows for, even celebrates, diversity—varied running styles at different paces—not prejudicial discrimination and rivalry. This is not just some ideal policy Paul promotes but a very practical one. Again, however advantaged and accomplished we appear to be, we're all destined to fall short and flat on our faces, and we need Christ and the entire running community to pick us up and spur us on. In fact, as the famous proverb warns, the prouder and more self-absorbed we are, the more likely we are to fall (Proverbs 16:18).

Running All Out in Christ

As previously mentioned, Paul is staunchly committed to running purposefully (not aimlessly) toward the goal line to gain a lasting reward (1 Corinthians 9:25-26). This does not, however, entail running a straight and narrow path. Life is more like a cross-country obstacle course over uncharted terrain. None of us knows what lies around the bend. But much is gained through the adventurous and often arduous process of life-running, provided we learn from faithful runners who have preceded us, team up with supportive current runners, and keep our eyes on the main goal and grand prize.

Paul, of course, aims to run his entire life-race in Christ. As "living is Christ" (Philippians 1:21), so running is Christ. Christ is the forerunning prototype, strengthening presence, driving purpose, and culminating prize. Paul runs "toward the goal... in Christ Jesus" that "[he] might gain Christ" (3:8, 14). The word for "gain" (*kerdainō*) has connotations of financial acquisition and social attainment, making money and boosting status. But Paul's Christ-oriented sense of "gain" is ironic and paradoxical. In no way does Paul try to earn Christ's favor, a fool's errand in any case, since Christ trades in an economy of gift over profit, grace over merit. So all the personal and social "gains" (*kerdē*) Paul had racked up count for nothing in his relationship with Christ (3:7), and living in Christ so transforms the normal order of things that even "dying is gain [*kerdos*]" (1:21).

Although Paul has no pretensions of earning his place on the Christ-track or reaching the goal line on his own strength, he does not simply coast along on Christ's coattails. Faith and works work in tandem. So do grace and grit. The Christ-race is not a spectator sport; it must be run with "athletic" discipline, focus, and energy. Thus Paul twice stresses his commitment to press on: "I press on to lay hold of that for which Christ has laid hold of me" (3:12); "I press on toward the goal...in Christ Jesus" (3:14). The repeated verb (*diōkō*) means "pursue, press on, push forward, stretch ahead." It signifies maximum engagement in a vital endeavor toward a valuable end. In running terms, it distinguishes a serious athlete from an occasional beach jogger.

Again, Paul trusts in Christ to reach the goal, not in his own willpower, and he freely admits, even with all his apostolic achievements, he has not yet "laid hold of" perfect Christlikeness (3:13). But he runs all out, striving, stretching, and straining toward Christ. And he's all in—in Christ—for whatever Christ has "laid hold of [him]" (3:12), including knocking him down, picking him up, dragging him along, and carrying him when necessary.

It's no accident that Paul also uses *diōkō* to refer to his former "persecuting" of Christ's church (3:6). In that context, Paul zealously "pressed on" to hunt down, seize, and prosecute believers in Christ. Remember, zeal can be virtuous or vicious depending on its goal. When Christ stopped him cold in his crusader track, he didn't squelch Paul's passionate drive but rather redirected it toward salutary ends. Still, however, it remained critical for Paul to temper his zeal with discerning "knowledge and full insight to help [him] determine what really matters" (1:9-10; cf. Romans 10:2) and with ever-mindful attention to Christ's leadership lest he "run in vain" (Philippians 2:16).

Running Toward Righteousness and Resurrection in Christ

While the consummate goal and gain of Paul's life-race is the "fullness" of Christ (Ephesians 1:23; Colossians 2:9-10), he focuses in Philippians 3 on two particular dimensions of Christ's life that he hopes to "gain": Christ's righteousness and resurrection (Philippians 3:7-11).

"Not Having a Righteousness of My Own"

In the roiling 1960s, "righteous" became a hip term for "excellent" or "real." In 1962, the popular vocal duo of Bobby Hatfield and Bill Medley came to be known as the Righteous Brothers, taking their cue from an audience member at a U.S. Marine base concert who shouted out at the end of the performance, "That was righteous, brothers!" In this context, "righteous" was similar to "cool," though not as enduring. I still routinely say, "That's cool," but it would be totally (totes) uncool to say, "That's righteous." Today, "righteous/righteousness" is reserved for pious religious talk and, even then, is rarely used in casual church conversation. "Bless you, brother/sister, for being so righteous" sounds stilted and strange. We still use "righteous" language in sermons and studies—it's a great biblical word—but often in a generic, superficial sense. Being "righteous" is a "good" thing, meriting an "Amen" or two but little analysis.

However, when Paul speaks about "righteousness" (*dikaiosynē*), as he often does in his letters, he speaks with deep meaning and motivation. He knows what he's talking about and wants to do. He aims to run a genuinely righteous race. Volumes have been written about the Bible's view of righteousness and Paul's in particular. Space does not permit a detailed discussion, but I highlight five key elements of Paul's perspective.

First, for Paul, righteousness is a practical experience, not a theoretical concept or rhetorical nicety. Righteousness is something someone has or doesn't have (3:9), something one feels, does, and is, a core part of one's character.

Second, Paul experiences righteousness as relational, actional, and evolutional: being in right relation with God and one another, doing the right thing—what God and Christ would do (WWJD?)—doing unto others as you would have them do unto you, helping put the world to rights, and pursuing "right paths" (Psalm 23:3) over the course of one's life.

Third, Paul's deep desire for righteousness is frustrated by his honest realization that he's unable to be wholly righteous on his own (Philippians 3:9). It's just not in him or in any of us self-centered humans, constantly entangled in mixed motives and personal agendas. Self-righteousness trades in arrogance and appearance, not in humility and reality. For Paul, the antidote to self-righteousness is Christ-righteousness, the righteousness "that comes through faith in Christ, the righteousness from God based on faith" (3:9).

Paul frequently links "righteousness" with "faith" (*pistis*), another religious word we throw around with fuzzy understanding. Common usage defines Christian faith as a set of tenets, doctrines, or beliefs (the faith) we profess about Christ's identity and ministry. While faith includes believing right things about Christ, it also involves entering into right relations of trust, commitment, and faithfulness toward Christ. And just as importantly, though often neglected, Christ-faith embraces Christ's own faithfulness, demonstrated in his loving devotion and action toward God, humanity, and all creation. It is Christ's living model of righteousness, extolled in the Philippians hymn (2:5-11), that sets the standard of excellence and endurance for running the race of life with his followers.

Fourth, Paul juxtaposes righteousness "that comes from the law" with righteousness "that comes through faith in Christ" (3:9). But juxtaposition does not mean opposition. Just as we must not pit faith against works, so we must not pit faith against law, specifically the Jewish law given by God to Israel, including the Ten Commandments and other scriptural teachings. Paul unequivocally states that "the law is holy, and the commandment is holy and just [righteous; *dikaia*] and good" (Romans 7:12). For a devout Jew like Paul, the law stands out as a great gift of God, guiding God's people in the way of life.

But the law itself has no inherent power to enforce compliance. The law certifies the covenant of love and grace "constituted" by God with God's people. Ideally, the people keep the law out of love and gratitude to God. More pragmatically, it's in their best interest to keep the law to avoid penalties for transgression (though the law also provides for pardons and making amends). But while the law enacts God's will, it cannot enable obedience by itself, any more than traffic laws and speeding tickets can enable safe driving. Encouragement, yes; enablement, no. Moreover, laws are always subject to selective interpretations and work-arounds.

As we've seen, Paul formerly convinced himself he was "blameless" in practicing "righteousness under the law" (Philippians 3:6). But his watershed encounter with Christ showed him the error of his ways, not the error of valuing the law (the law was not to blame), but the error of missing the true loving and liberating "spirit" of the law and the renewed ways and means of fulfilling the law through the power of God's Spirit and Christ's resurrected life (2 Corinthians 3:1-18).

Fifth, I suggest summarizing Paul's attitude toward righteousness as "confident humility," an idea I picked up from organizational psychologist Adam Grant in *Think Again: The Power of Knowing What You Don't Know*,[1] which has nothing to do with biblical study but aptly applies to Paul in Philippians. Over the course of his life, Paul "gained" humility and came to know what he didn't know (and have) before, namely, true righteousness in Christ. He admitted he was wrong and reoriented his life around "the surpassing value of knowing Christ Jesus my Lord" (Philippians 3:8), who "humbled himself and became obedient [did the 'right' thing] to the point of death" (2:8). However, this prime "righteous" virtue of humility associated with self-giving and sacrifice does not entail self-loathing and helplessness. Paul came to know he was a "sinner" of the worst order because of his former career as a zealous persecutor in God's name (3:6; cf. 1 Timothy 1:12-16).

But Paul stopped short of labeling himself or anyone else as a "wretch" or "worm." (Old hymns, still sung in some circles, profess Christ's salvation for "a wretch like me" and "such a worm as I.")

Indeed, Paul merges considered confidence with healthy humility. By no means confident that he's right all the time, he's nonetheless confident in his humility to stay open to course corrections and press through missteps. Again, adapting Adam Grant's insight to Paul's philosophy of racing, Paul and fellow runners in Christ are "determined to reach the correct answer [goal] in the long run, and they know that means they have to be open to stumbling, backtracking, and rerouting in the short run."[2] Yes, but don't miss Paul's open secret of humble confidence (trust, faith) in God's unfailing purpose and energy: "I am confident of this, that the one [God] who began a good [righteous] work in you [and me] will continue to complete it until the day of Jesus Christ (Philippians 1:6; cf. 2:13).

"The Power of His Resurrection"

The power of God that fuels Paul's right-oriented race is the same power that raised Christ from the dead, the creative power of divine life. That's as powerful as it gets in Paul's universe. But the benefit of energizing power (not dominating force) requires access to that power in sufficient amounts. A massive power plant across the street is of no use if my house isn't wired to receive electricity. Hoping that Christ's resurrection power is not simply held in reserve for when we drop dead at the finish line and need a high-voltage jump start to everlasting life, how can we runners on Team Christ tap into this power now, in this life?

In first-century Jewish thought, "the resurrection from the dead" commonly referred to the general resurrection of all people at the end of the age to face final judgment. The hope was for a blessed resurrection to eternal life. In Paul's running terms, this is the goalpost he presses toward hopefully—and humbly—"if somehow I may attain the resurrection from the dead. Not that I have already obtained [it] or have already reached [this] goal" (3:11-12). The adverbs "somehow" and "not already" carry a lot of weight here, tempering cocksure certainty with honest humility.

But there's more to Paul's running strategy, namely, a creative tension between what is already available and what is not or, more simply, between "already" (in part) and "not yet" (in full). This recalls our discussion about living in "thin places" between life and death, earth and heaven, where life breaks through death and heaven breaks into earth as foretastes of the coming "thick" convergence of a new heaven and earth. Recall that Paul contends that "our citizenship is [already] in heaven," even while we wait for Christ's climactic transformation of our finite bodies into his resurrected likeness (3:20-21). This remarkable comment comes on the heels of Paul's running analogy. Team Christ runs on earth under the banner of heaven, fueled by the same Spirit who raised Jesus from the dead.

But this side of the grand finish line, when God will perfectly merge earthly and heavenly realms, runners must regularly refill their tanks and recharge their batteries. One can only go so far—depending on running style, road conditions, weather effects, traffic patterns—before running out of gas or electricity, as we say in our motorized culture. The rougher the journey, the more often we need to refuel. Spirit-filling, like filling our bodies with food and drink, is not a once-for-all experience but a recurring life habit. Ephesians 5:18 urges, "Keep being filled with the Spirit" (my translation). In this life, we are called to keep pressing through myriad challenges and hardships, even unto death—as Christ did—with regular Spirit pit stops.

The race of life is a series of trial runs—running through trials—with the crucified-risen Christ. Notice how tightly Paul links experiencing "the power of [Christ's] resurrection" with "the sharing of his sufferings by becoming like him in his death, if somehow I may attain the resurrection from the dead" (Philippians 3:10-11). Crucifixion and resurrection are a package deal. Paul purposefully runs under the "weak" power of Christ's cross in fellowship with weak and ailing sufferers, drawing on "strong" currents of the risen Christ's energy until God's final turbocharge of eternal life. Accordingly, Paul is not running away from earthly obstacles and entanglements toward Christ's outstretched heavenly arms but running arm in arm with the crucified-risen Christ, finding grace, strength, love, and joy along the way toward realizing fullness of life in Christ.

Heaven is not the distant goal of the Christ-centered race but rather a part of present earthly experience ("on earth as it is in heaven"), a promissory note or "down payment" on the full merger of God's heavenly and earthly creations (2 Corinthians 1:20-22; 5:4-5). What then of Paul's statement in Philippians 3:14: "I press on toward the goal, toward the prize of the heavenly call in Christ Jesus"? That seems like heaven is the main goal and prize. Yes, it would if that's what Paul actually said. Here, however, I take issue with the NRSVue translation. I'm not alone. The Greek word is not the standard term for "heavenly" (*ouranios*) but instead a common adverb meaning "above, up, upward" (*anō*), as the NRSVue acknowledges in a footnote. The RSV, NASB, and CEB, among other modern versions, read "upward call." That's better, though I prefer the simpler "high calling" (KJV). Again, this "prize" is not the calling of Christ to heaven, but Christ's high, noble calling itself. The top prize is the high calling.

Still, we wonder, what is Christ calling Paul to? In Paul's writings, "call/calling" is primarily associated with vocation, the life and work one feels called to live and do, one's life mission. For Paul, the mission call that matters most comes from God. He stresses in Galatians 1:15-16, "The one [God] . . . set me apart before I was born and called me through his grace was pleased to reveal his Son [Jesus Christ] to me, so that I might proclaim him." While this call to preach is particular to Paul's career, he believes that all God's people are called to live and work on this earth as God's people, demonstrating God's right-making character and purpose in the world:

> *I, therefore, the prisoner in the Lord, beg you [all] to walk in a manner worthy of the calling to which you have been called, with humility and gentleness, with patience, bearing with one another in love, making every effort to maintain the unity of the Spirit in the bond of peace: there is one body and one Spirit, just as you were called to the one hope of your calling.*
>
> *(Ephesians 4:1-4)*

There's the same emphasis on practical living (walking, running) in a manner worthy of the Lord that Paul stresses in Philippians 1:27, and throughout this letter, in a Spirit of humility, gentleness, love, and peace (1:8-9; 2:1-8; 4:1-7)—"weak" qualities by worldly standards but the vital means of Christ's saving power. That's the redemptive race we're called to run here and now, day in and day out, stretching with every fiber of our being to fulfill.

CHAPTER 6

The Strength of Christ

Key Passage

Philippians 4:1-14

In some churches today, Christians are encouraged to adopt a Bible "life verse" that is especially meaningful to them and suitable as a life-guiding motto. Philippians is a popular source for these pithy philosophies of life. "For to me, living is Christ" (1:21) makes a nice life verse, not least because it neatly encapsulates Paul's own philosophy of life.

The last chapter of this letter also has its gems. I've long been drawn to Philippians 4:6-7 (okay, that's two verses) that affirms "the peace of God, which surpasses all understanding." I memorized this text in Sunday school, and it's stuck with me ever since. But arguably the letter's most well-known, frequently chosen life verse is Philippians 4:13—"I can do all things through [Christ] who strengthens me." (Technically, the text uses the pronoun "him," but this clearly refers to Christ.) Again, this is a deeply personal conviction for Paul, borne out of his experience "in any and all circumstances." It constitutes the open secret of robust living Paul claims to have learned (4:12).

Though the Greek term rendered, "I have learned the secret of" (*memyēmai*), could apply to initiation rites into various ancient mystery religions, Paul does not set up Philippians 4:13 as a magical formula or mantra for Christian service: "Chant 'I can do all things through Christ who strengthens me' for ten minutes five times a day and all will be well." Nor, to update the context, is this Paul's version of the power of positive thinking or *The Little Engine That Could*: "I can do all things, I can do all things, I think I can, I think can—with Christ as my Engineer."

As we've repeatedly seen, Paul encourages thinking about one's life in relationship to Christ, having "the same mind... that was in Christ Jesus" (2:5). But this is about deep thinking and reflection, not rote recitation. It's about mindful, experiential learning over the course of one's life in Christ. Bridging the promise of peace in Philippians 4:6-7 and the profession of strength in 4:10-14 is the call to "think" about what really matters: "whatever is true, whatever is honorable, whatever is just, whatever is pure, whatever is pleasing, whatever is commendable, if there is any excellence and anything worthy of praise" (4:8). Such virtues, however, are not merely noble ideas for contemplative musing but practical goals for active learning, as Paul tries to model in imitation of Christ: "As for the things that you have learned and received and heard and noticed in me, do them" (4:9).

This term for "learned" (*manthanō*) also appears two verses later: "I learned to be content with whatever I have" (4:11). Though distinct from "learn the secret of" (4:12), this word shares a similar educational orientation. Specifically, *manthanō* connotes active learning as a "disciple" (*mathētē*) of an esteemed mentor. A disciple is fundamentally a lifelong learner and faithful follower of a master teacher. Of course, for Paul and associates, that model mentor is the Lord Jesus Christ. In Christ's curriculum, peace and contentment do not come so much in flashes of insight or mind-numbing techniques as in the disciplined (discipled) processes of working out one's salvation (2:12) throughout the challenging journey with Christ. In modern psychological lingo, we might call this Christ-centered cognitive-behavioral therapy supporting a growth mindset.

But this cognitive/mental perspective must not be separated from vital affective/emotional influences. Scientific research increasingly shows the dynamic interconnection between thoughts (cognitions) and feelings (emotions) in human experience. Long before neuroscience brain imaging and professional psychology studies, Paul had a deft intuitive grasp of the interplay of "hearts and minds" (4:7) in life development, which for him meant spiritual formation in Christ. Learning is as emotional as it is informational; indeed, emotions provide valuable information about who we are and what we want. Emotions move us, and motivate us to pursue matters of prime importance, matters of life and death. To be sure, their very energy makes them unpredictable: Emotions can get the best of us, as we say, overwhelming and misleading us, or they can bring out the best in us, propelling us toward flourishing life.

It's in this latter sense that Paul links his confidence and contentment in Christ's strength amid life's ups and downs with positive emotional resources, especially joy and peace. And as always, Paul's experience of Christ-centered strength is vitally connected to his communal network of supportive partners: "In any case, it was kind of you [Philippian believers] to share in my distress" (4:14). "Share" is a compound form of *koinōneō*, emphasizing sharing together in mutual compassion and concern.

Strength in the Joyous Confidence of Christ

Proportionally, no writing of Paul highlights joy/rejoicing more than Philippians. In chapter 2, we saw how Paul envelops this letter with harmonious keynotes of rejoicing (*chairō*) and thanksgiving (*eucharisteō*) concerning the Philippians' support of prisoner Paul (1:3-11; 4:10-20). Their material "gifts" sent to Paul via Epaphroditus enabled him to survive his ordeal of isolation.

But joy is not simply an apt emotional response to receiving vital care. Joy itself, with and beyond thanksgiving, has strengthening effects, not least during trying times. During the challenging period of reconstructing Judahite society after Babylon's devastating assault on the region, Ezra, the leading priest buoyed the beleaguered people by proclaiming, "The joy of the LORD is your strength" (Nehemiah 8:10). Joy defines godly strength and power. God-centered joy generates gracious strength and inspires humble confidence, as opposed to hate and bitterness that fuel oppressive power and blustery arrogance.

Significantly, Paul prefaces his advice about finding peace and strength to cope with anxiety and distress (Philippians 4:6-14) with the double call, "Rejoice in the Lord always; again I will say, Rejoice," qualified by, "Let your gentleness be known to everyone" (4:4-5). This joy is no less strong for its gentleness. It's a calm, considered joy pulsing with "clean energy" and steady strength through the roiling storms of life. With a nod to Ezra, we might adapt Paul's motto in Philippians 4:13: "I can do all things through [the joy of Christ] who strengthens me."

And applying Paul's philosophy more widely, Jürgen Moltmann commends Christianity as a "unique religion of joy" in which "joy is the strength for living, the empowerment to love, the delight in a creative beginning. It wakes us up and makes us alive from within."[1] That's quite a claim, which Moltmann does not make flippantly but in full awareness, with Paul, of terrible suffering in the world, epitomized in the flesh, bone, and blood of the crucified-risen Jesus. Christ-centered joy in pain and anguish is not some perverse self-beating impulse but a profound sense of God's purposeful, potent life-stream in Christ coursing through all circumstances, bad and good: a dynamic interflow of death and life, crucifixion-and-resurrection (see 3:10).

If joy is so important to robust living in Christ, it merits more careful investigation, both in terms of what joy means from Paul's perspective and who feels and sparks joy. We've begun to touch on these key questions. Now we take a deeper dive.

What Is Joy?

Whatever joy is, it's a good thing, a highly desirable feeling, mindset, and mode of being. We know that much, and so do advertisers.

Highlighting a product's joyous essence is sure to pique people's interest. Any candy worth its sugar offers a sweet experience, but Almond Joy® is special. You want to take the drudgery out of dishwashing by hand? Just use the dishwashing liquid Joy®, and revel in dipping your hands every evening in sudsy ecstasy. (I prefer Dawn's® delivery of awesome awakening, but to each their own.) Joysticks make video games more thrilling, and joyriding soups up car cruising.

Such commodifying of joy is miles and millennia away from Paul's concept. The joy of Christ that sustains and strengthens Paul through "all things" is not based in "things" one has or doesn't have. The popular Japanese organizer Marie Kondo would agree that "one's life does not consist in the abundance of possessions" (that's Jesus in Luke 12:15) but rather in a limited number of valued things that "spark joy."[2] That's a better approach to life than unbridled consumerism but still not what inspires Paul. His experience of joyous living, while including gratitude for material things, transcends these things: "I know what it is to have little, and I know what it is to have plenty," to be "well-fed" and to go "hungry" (Philippians 4:12). And through it all, including confinement in a jail cell, joyous confidence and peaceful contentment fortify him in body and spirit.

Further, it's useful to distinguish joy as a core emotional attitude from happiness, even while recognizing their overlaps. Single emotion terms help us gain an initial handle on our feelings so we might begin to manage them properly. But as rippling fluid processes, emotions outstrip one-word labels. They slip and slide, swirl and swell together in a running stream of mixed feelings, better reflected in lively narratives (the story of Christ!) and allusive poems (the Christ hymn!) that appreciate emotions' dynamic force field. Still, words are building blocks of understanding, including emotional understanding, and they accrue different shades of meaning. Accordingly, "joy" and "happiness" have somewhat different emotional vibes that enable us to track the dimensions of Paul's joy in Philippians more precisely. For example, joy

(1) lasts longer, (2) runs deeper, and (3) extends wider and (4) higher than happiness.

"Happy hours" promise temporary anesthetic relief from a hard day's work. Joy is more durable and sustainable. It works in the long run. As Paul opens the letter praying "with joy" concerning God's "good work" among the Philippians "from the first day until now... until the [final] day of Jesus Christ" (1:3-6) and their continued "progress and joy in faith" (1:25), so Paul ends the letter emphasizing joy as a constant source of strength: "Keep rejoicing in the Lord always; again I will say, Keep rejoicing" (4:4, my translation). Joy takes the long view, trusting in the sure, even if sometimes slow, outworking of God's good purposes.

Joy also takes a deep dive into the tangled realities of life, unlike happiness, which often skims the surface of shallow waters. Resisting the cheap cosmetics of "putting on a happy face," joy motivates robust courage to grapple with hard questions and tough situations in the quest for creative solutions. Scarcely known for their happy-go-lucky dispositions, Greek and Roman Stoic teachers still allowed for virtuous emotions or "good passions" (*eupatheia*) regulated by sound reason. Chief among these wise emotions is joy, defined as "rational elation" (Diogenes Laertius), "when the mind is moved quietly and consistently according to reason" (Cicero). If you've ever lost yourself in the flow of studying something that really grabbed your interest, you know the stimulating joy that drives and derives from this experience: the joy of learning, the joy of discovery. In-depth Bible study can bring such joy, not least a study of Philippians, whose author ponders joy as the passionate mindset of Christ, motivating flourishing life.

Building on its long and deep foundations are joy's third and fourth dimensions: its wide-angle and high-altitude worldview. A common trend in modern happiness studies is to track people's assessments of "subjective well-being" in response to push notifications on their cell phones. Message: How are you feeling now on a happiness scale from 1 to 5? Click your response. Obviously, numbers will vary after a delicious lunch and then an hour later after a boring committee meeting. But over an extended period, a happiness average or "set point" emerges. This information is useful to a point, but it suffers from overvaluing how much happiness can be objectively quantified by subjective reporting. Moreover, feelings of happiness tend to be narrowly circumstantial and personalized: How does this momentary event affect me? In any case, it's hard to imagine Paul tracking his happiness pulse in prison or anywhere else.

Joy, by contrast, thrives in states of awe, wonder, and elation at the vast, multivarious universe encompassing us. Joy sees the big picture, as big as all creation. As Paul is physically bound in chains and a cell, he also joyfully participates in Christ's boundless cosmic-creational story (2:6-11). Joy is not the absence and elimination of suffering but the transcendence and elevation of all life within a wider and higher framework.

And most important for Paul, that joyous framework is relational through and through.

Who Is Joy?

This question may sound awkward, but in fact, for Paul, joy is less an entity one has than an identity one is—a social-relational identity. The "in the Lord" modifier of "Rejoice" (4:4) does not associate joy with the Lord to give it a pious veneer distinguished from more mundane enjoyments, like a child's birthday party or an Easter egg hunt. Let's not forget "in Christ" is Paul's shorthand for a long, deep, intimate relationship with, for, and on account of the living Christ, measuring everything against "the surpassing value of knowing Christ Jesus my Lord" (3:8) (By the way, I think the child-welcoming and child-identifying Christ [Mark 9:36-37] would joyously celebrate birthday parties and Easter egg hunts.) The "joy of the Lord" himself—the Lord God of Israel (Nehemiah 8:10) and the Lord Jesus Christ (John 15:11; 17:13 ["my joy"])—is Paul's strength.

But this is not some private secret of joy but rather joy that Paul gladly shares with his Philippian kin in Christ, who also are the joy of Paul's life: "My brothers and sisters, whom I love and long for, my joy and crown" (Philippians 4:1). Again, joy is rooted in relational experience, not in transactional exchange. Although the Philippians have reciprocated Paul's gospel ministry with material gifts, the Christ-joy that binds them together is not a contingent business arrangement but an inherent component of loving, longing fellowship.

Paul's joyous reward, my "crown," is not the stuff his admirers give him but the very life he shares with generous partners in Christ. He writes in a similar vein to the Thessalonian congregation: "For [who] is our hope or joy or crown of boasting before our Lord Jesus at his coming? Is it not you [all]? Yes, you are our glory and joy!" (1 Thessalonians 2:19-20). And not only at Jesus's final "coming," Paul would certainly add, but at every moment until then.

Further, it must be said, the joyous life Paul shares with the Philippian and Thessalonian believers is not some utopian state of bliss but rather a joy-fortified struggle through life's marathon that includes challenging one another and working through conflicts that inevitably arise. The same Paul who calls his parishioners "my joy" has no problem calling them to account when they falter and urging them to "live your life in a manner worthy of the gospel of Christ" (Philippians 1:27; see 1:27–2:16; 4:2-3; 1 Thessalonians 4:1-12).

Perhaps the best illustration we have of a personal-relational experience of joy is the (healthy) parent–child bond, which need not be restricted to biological ties. Paul refers to himself as both father and mother to spiritual offspring in Christ's family (Galatians 4:19; Philippians 2:22; 1 Thessalonians 2:7-12; Philemon 10-16). It's common to hear a parent say that a beloved daughter or son is "such a joy," "the joy of my life." Even allowing for some gushy sentimentality and squishy idealism, this expression of joy has a strong ring of authenticity and a dose of reality. We know our little darlings can be selfish monsters who run us ragged, take more than they give, and are not beyond disappointing us and breaking our hearts. Back to the happiness issue, some studies suggest that those who have kids, though happy enough, do not measure quite as happy as voluntarily childless couples. Still, with all the overwhelming risk and responsibility of child-rearing, with all the sleepless nights and endless frets, there's something awesome, in the deepest sense, about little ones themselves and our developing bond with them that brings indescribable joy.

Just look at the father in Jesus's famous parable who can't help longing for the return of his wayward, wasteful son. Then, when the son finally comes home, instead of demanding an apology and exacting punishment, the father runs toward him, hugs, kisses, clothes, and throws him a big "welcome home" party. It's celebration time. The joy of my life has returned (Luke 15:11-32; cf. 15:6-7, 9-10).

Strength in the Peaceful Contentment of Christ

In modern America, the relationship between peace and strength typically concerns matters of national security. A popular slogan touts "Peace Through Strength." That is, if you want to be safe and secure, you must have superior might and firepower to deter would-be attackers and defend yourself when they attack. At all costs, you must lead the arms race: bigger biceps, harder fists, higher-powered guns and ammo, more lethal missiles. Might makes right.

But does it make peace? Does it bring a whole, deep, rich sense of internal (within) and interrelational (between) well-being, like that associated with the Hebrew concept of shalom? Hardly. The pressure to outgun opposing forces stems from and stirs up fear and anxiety. How do you know you've covered all the security bases to fend off surprise assaults? If you have a basic home security system and a handgun in a nightstand, is that enough? Maybe you need a systems upgrade and a few more weapons to protect against stealthy and well-armed invaders? When is enough, enough? It's a scary world out there. The increasing prospect of nuclear annihilation since World War II has scarcely achieved world peace, to say nothing of peace of mind. Growing up during the height of the Cold War with regular drills to duck and tuck under school desks did not make me feel calmer, any more than today's children feel less stress with routine drills to deal with crazed school shooters toting automatic rifles.

I do not say this to argue for particular public and international policies. I'm not qualified to make those decisions and recognize how difficult they can be. I simply observe that strategies to enforce peace by the threat or use of violent power threaten to undermine the goal of peace. A constant arms race is stressful and exhausting, not peaceful and restoring. And recalling the theme of the previous chapter, an arms race is not the race Christ calls Paul and company to run.

Paul is no more a war department official or state department diplomat than I am. His "fellow soldier" description of Epaphroditus in Philippians 2:25 is purely figurative. Paul has no illusions, which would be nothing more than preposterous delusions, of fighting his way out of his Roman prison, raising an army to defeat Rome's legions, or persuading Caesar to lay down his arms, give up his empire, and peacefully coexist with all peoples. Paul is fully aware of Caesar's august authority and military might, not to mention vexing threats from various local opposers and "enemies" of Christ (1:28; 3:18).

But what about Paul's confidence in the colossal power of God and Christ? God and Christ are greater than all the Roman gods and Caesar, right? God and Christ have the whole cosmic heavenly host at their command. Yes, but they have an altogether different attitude toward power than earthly rulers who think they're gods and messiahs. If I may put it baldly, God and Christ are not power-mad egomaniacs. They are secure enough in their sovereign positions to cede self-obsessed interests and serve the weak and lowly. Remember the heart of the Christ hymn-story. Christ does not cling to his supreme divine power station but embodies extreme human weakness, "taking the form of a slave" in solidarity with the most vulnerable people, "to the point of death—even death on a cross" (2:6-8). No summoning a twelve-legion angelic strike force, which he has every divine right to do (Matthew 26:53). Strength and power to save the world come through weakness and service.

To be sure, Paul envisions the exalted Christ's powerful return to earth to complete the grand world-saving, right-making, peace-fulfilling project (Philippians 1:6; 3:21). But in the meantime, God's people are called to learn how to live like Christ in peace and contentment within ourselves and between one another, whatever the circumstances. The goal is to become instruments of God's peace and goodwill here and now, befitting the peace-full, perfected world to come. We are to blaze the path of true peace and security amid life's myriad challenges, not peddle the cheap panaceas of bogus "strongmen." Paul has no patience with power brokers who trumpet "Peace and Security" but only intend it for themselves at the expense of those who need it most (1 Thessalonians 5:3) or with callous charlatans who cry, "'Peace, peace,' / when there is no peace" (Jeremiah 6:14).

Recall that Paul urges his Philippian friends to contemplate "whatever is true" (Philippians 4:8). So, what is Paul's understanding of the true "peace of God" and "God of peace" that soothes and strengthens "hearts and minds in Christ Jesus" (4:7-9)?

Peace That Surmounts Disagreement

Paul starts his peace talk in Philippians 4 by addressing two congregational leaders who have fallen out with each other for some unspecified reason. It doesn't matter to Paul why they're discordant; nothing justifies turning against one another and troubling the whole fellowship. Moreover, if leaders fail to model peaceful unity, they disrupt the peace mission not only inside the struggling community but also outside to a fractured world.

Paul calls out two women ministers: "I urge Euodia and I urge Syntyche to be of the same mind in the Lord" (4:2). By saying each one's name, Paul shows his respect for these women's notable standing in the community. While their disagreement is a source of concern for Paul, it doesn't disqualify them from leadership. Paul neither demands their dismissal nor demeans their dispute as a petty squabble. Paul knows these women's dedication from personal experience, "for they have struggled beside me in the work of the gospel" (4:3). Notice Paul does not pull rank and say they worked "under me" or "for me." As surely as Timothy and Epaphroditus are Paul's "coworkers" (2:22, 25), so are Euodia and Syntyche. In Philippians 4:3, Paul uses two compound verbal forms with the prefix *syn-* to describe the women's coequal cooperation with Paul and other servants of Christ: *synēthlēsan* ("struggling together" like athletes) and *synergōn* ("working together" in synergy).

Because Paul values Euodia and Syntyche so highly, it no doubt pains him to hear about their clash. But more than that, Paul would worry about the ripple effect of their unresolved conflict on the peace and security of the vulnerable flock these women shepherd. The strength of the fellowship depends on having "the same mind in the Lord" (4:2; cf. 2:5), the same fundamental disposition to think, feel, and act in a Christ-focused way, standing firm together to serve common interests and withstand common difficulties (cf. 1:17–2:4).

Such unity does not require uniformity. Like-mindedness does not require absolute single-mindedness, insisting that everyone think and say the same things, like robots and parrots. That's the aim of insecure authoritarian regimes based on fear monitored by unthinking "thought police," not peaceful communitarian bodies based on trust, freedom, and mutual accountability—like the body of the Servant-Lord Jesus Christ. This is the ideal body in Paul's view, comprised of many different members, each gifted in their own ways (Romans 12:3-8; 1 Corinthians 12:4-31) yet working together in "the unity of the Spirit [and] in the bond of peace" (Ephesians 4:3-4) under the gracious "rule" of "the peace of Christ" (Colossians 3:15). That's strength through peace, not the other way around.

Along with making a direct public appeal to Euodias and Syntyche (Philippians is an open congregational letter, not a private memo) to renew their collaborative ministry, Paul also enlists a trusted friend, "my loyal companion," to "help these women" (Philippians 4:3). This is not to suggest that Paul shows his true patriarchal colors by sending "my loyal" male lieutenant to get these cantankerous church ladies in line, as if to imply they were somehow being disloyal to Paul. His commendation of Euodia and Syntyche as faithful mission partners stands firm.

Further, I don't think "my loyal companion" is the best translation. I prefer the RSV's "true yokefellow," even with its older language. There's no possessive "my" pronoun in Greek here (as if Paul regarded this associate as "my guy"), and the "loyal" term (*gnēsie*) also means "true" or "genuine," as in Paul's touting Timothy as one "genuinely [*gnēsiōs*] concerned" about the Philippians' well-being (2:20). In short, Paul applies no loyalty test, pitting a crony comrade against Euodia and Syntyche. That would go against Paul's fervent commitment to unity and mutual service.

Finally, the "companion" term (*syzyge*) literally means "one yoked-together" or "yokefellow." This image comes from the premodern farming practice of plowing fields with oxen teams harnessed by iron or wooden yokes. Yoking means working, working in tandem, working together peacefully toward a common goal. Paul's "yokefellow" thus typifies Paul's shared view of ministry on Team Christ, including women like Euodia and Syntyche and men like himself, this unnamed yokefellow (unless his actual name is Syzyge, as some scholars suggest), Clement (otherwise unknown), Timothy, Epaphroditus, and a host of other "coworkers" yoked together under Christ's gentle headship (see Matthew 11:29-30 on Christ's "gentle and humble yoke"). Such partners in Christ are certified life-givers and life-savers, registered in God's "book of life" (Philippians 4:3).

Peace That Surpasses Understanding

Accompanying active social and ministerial facets of Christ-centered peace are more contemplative personal and psychological factors. Christian spirituality has a long tradition of emphasizing both contemplation and action, prayer and service—ideally as complementary but sometimes as competitive forms of devotion. Paul strives to balance the two.

Paul knows one of the surest ways to stifle loving action toward others is through self-preoccupied anxiety. The more we worry about our own well-being, the less inclined we are to aid other sufferers, particularly those outside our inner circles. Anxiety pulls us inward and fills our mindscapes. While there's merit to putting our problems in perspective by pushing ourselves to help others with their struggles, that only takes us so far. Strong emotions like fear and anxiety cannot simply be willed away or shoved aside. Emotions provide vital information about the state of our lives that we ignore or repress at our peril. Best to lean into emotions, accept the feelings they evoke, ponder what they teach us, and then act accordingly: Feel–Think–Do.

As previously mentioned, Paul counsels the Philippians to think (4:8) and do (4:9) the things that make for godly peace. But what about the feeling part? Paul begins his peace talk with a strong injunction against anxiety: "Do not be anxious about anything" (4:6). The Greek word order accentuates the sweeping nature of this mandate: "In-no-way [*mēden*] be anxious." Further, the grammar suggests Paul implores his people to quit the bad habit of anxiety they've already developed, effectively pleading, "Stop being so anxious about everything all the time. Stop being such a worrywart!"

Although Paul acknowledges the Philippians' anxious feelings, he doesn't accept them. He frankly doesn't seem very sympathetic at this point. To say curtly, "Stop feeling all those anxious feelings," seems like an insensitive command. You can't just flick an off switch or pull the plug on anxiety. In fact, the more you worry about worrying, the more worried you get!

We should not forget, however, that Paul earlier expressed his grateful solidarity with the Philippians for their "same struggle" with various physical, psychological, social, material, and religious challenges (1:29-30). And Paul later echoes this sentiment in 4:3 (Euodia and Syntyche "have struggled beside me") and 4:14 ("It was kind of you [all] to share my distress")—verses that closely surround the "no anxiety" directive in 4:6. Thus, we should consider that Paul has more to say about dealing with peace-robbing anxiety than a flat "Just say no." Indeed, he doesn't stop with "Stop being anxious" but proceeds to explain how his Philippian siblings in Christ might move through their anxiety to a more serene, secure mode of being.

Despite his "Stop!" warning, Paul mounts no campaign to eradicate anxiety, as if he could or should. Anxiety is an innate part of human experience with beneficial functions of alerting us to potential threats and motivating us to take suitable precautions. If I'm anxious about a persistent pain in my body, that can be a helpful spur to seek medical attention. Anxiety about every little twitch and tingle, however, can spiral into obsessive hypochondria. The key is balanced emotional regulation. It's not surprising in our increasingly angry and anxious age, fostered by rapid social and technological change, that the market is flooded with anger management and anxiety coping courses, books, and advice columns. Paul is no psychologist, therapist, or self-help guru, but within his Christ-centered worldview, he offers wise counsel about cultivating a strong sense of peace and contentment in anxious situations.

Consider three key aspects of Paul's peace talk in Philippians 4:6-7: (1) praying with thanksgiving, (2) surpassing all understanding, and (3) guarding hearts and minds.

First, Paul enjoins his anxious Philippians friends, "In everything by prayer and supplication with thanksgiving let your requests be made known to God" (4:6). He urges prayerful contemplation before haphazard action. Anxiety tends to prompt rash responses and overreactions. Prayer slows down the process and provides a critical perspective, extending beyond depressive thinking ("Woe is me") to expansive thanksgiving ("Thanks be to God"). This is not mind-tricking denial of pain and suffering but rather mindful affirmation of blessings and opportunities that continue to abound in life.

While a thankful spirit tempers anxieties about what we think we lack now or will lose soon, it's not simply content to accept things as they are and will be without seeking changes. Accordingly, Paul's view of prayer supplements thanksgiving with petition, appreciation with asking God to ease our anxieties by altering our circumstances and supplying much-needed resources (4:19): "Let your requests be made known to God" (4:6).

This is not, however, to treat prayer as placing a list of items in some heavenly "cart" for God to ship to us via Angel Express (free of charge for "prime" members). That's shopping, not praying. That's transactional business, not relational partnership with God. We're invited to share our burdens with God and Christ, knowing they will respond with solidarity and sympathy. But not necessarily with the kind of relief we request. Notice that Paul does not promise that our requested orders will be filled.

Paul knew this all too well from his experience of pleading to the Lord three times to remove a torturous, satanic "thorn" in his "flesh"—to no avail. We don't know what this "thorn" was, other than no actual botanical barb. But whatever it was, it severely hurt Paul's body, and he wanted to be rid of it! But God had other ideas. This "thorn," Paul learned, though "a messenger of Satan," would be used by God to keep Paul humble and teach him that paradoxical Christ-principle of strength through weakness (2 Corinthians 12:7-10). Not an easy "point" to grasp, but one that follows from Christ's own suffering on a splintery cross with a crown of real thorns sticking into his head.

Though not guaranteeing satisfaction of specific prayer requests, Paul adds a second plank to his peace plan, namely, that prayer channels the very peace of God that surpasses normal human understanding (4:7). Paul does not suddenly shift into some spacey mindless mode after all his emphasis on thoughtful "knowledge and full insight" (1:9). As with joy, peace combines affective and cognitive elements, prompting Paul to speak of God's peace permeating "your hearts and minds" (Philippians 4:7). The notion of surpassing understanding does not mean bypassing, still less trespassing, rational understanding. It means going beyond narrow concepts, in this case misconceptions of peace, such as the absence of conflict (that's numb inertia, not robust peace) or the presence of brute strength (that's forced dominance, not reconciling peace).

As with the strong joy of the Lord, the strong peace of the Lord is most keenly felt by contemplating the awesome expanse of God's creative, evolving universe that exceeds our limited understanding. As James Taylor's song "The Secret O' Life" says, even "Einstein said he could never understand it all."[3] To a cynical mind, such honest humility could lead to resigned despair: What's the use in trying to make good sense of an unfathomable world? But to a hopeful mind aligned with the mind of Christ, honest humility in the face of infinite mystery inspires open curiosity to keep growing in understanding, especially concerning "the things that make for peace" (Luke 19:42; Romans 14:19). And the more we pursue the peace of Christ, the more we perceive the strength of this peace radiating throughout and "ruling" over (Colossians 3:15) our hearts and minds.

Third, Paul envisions the strength of God's peace in protective terms, *guarding our hearts and minds in Christ Jesus* (see Philippians 4:7). Note again, however, that Paul does not view stockpiling defensive matériel as a means to peace but rather that peace itself is the defense. The peace of God-in-Christ stands guard between adverse influences and circumstances around us and our feelings and thoughts about them.

Notably, Paul's "guard" (*phroreuō*) image trades on a term applied to military or prison guards, like those stationed to watch Paul during his present custody. So the peace of God, surpassing all understanding, is like a prison guard? That sounds more restraining than strengthening. Peace through chains? Yes, in a couple of senses. In one sense, Paul reaffirms that living in Christ affords peace in prison, despite his chains. But in another sense, Paul suggests that Christ-centered peace has a legitimate guard role itself as a checkpoint of information and perceptions between us and the world, a security screener separating harmful and helpful elements.

Recall that Paul's current prison guards allowed Epaphroditus to bring aid to Paul from the Philippians and to bear Paul's letter out to them (2:25-30; 4:18) and that "the whole imperial guard" proved receptive to his testimony about Christ (1:13; 4:22). All of this served the interests of peace among Paul, Philippian believers, and supportive Roman agents and strengthened them in their shared struggles. Such peace is by no means painless or mindless. But it feels and thinks through crises in dynamic relation with the crucified-risen Christ, guided—and guarded—by a Christ-suffused philosophy of life surpassing conventional understanding.

AFTERWORD

We've Got a Summons

Paul's secret of life in Philippians is not a program, principle, or pill (red or otherwise) but rather the person of the Lord Jesus Christ. "Living is Christ" (1:21). Living is a dynamic relationship with Christ throughout the rigorous course ("race") of fragile mortal life toward the goal of full Christ-life and Christ-likeness. Christ is both the model and means, the pattern and power, of flourishing life: "Let the same mind[set] be in you that was in Christ Jesus" (2:5). "I can do all things through [Christ] who strengthens me" (4:13). Simply put, with a few simple slogans or "life verses" to clinch the deal.

But not so simple to put into practice. Not by the Philippian believers Paul wrote to, who wouldn't have needed this letter if they had everything in order, and not even by Paul himself, who admits varying degrees of anxiety concerning his fate as a prisoner (1:19-26), the health and status of his beloved "brother" Epaphroditus (2:25-30), his prospect of "attain[ing] resurrection from the dead" (3:10-12), and his vulnerability to "being in need" and unduly dependent on the Philippians' charity (4:10-13).

To be sure, Paul's primary tone in this letter is hopeful, optimistic, and confident because of his trust in the faithful Christ. Paul's positive contentment (not passive resignation) in confinement constitutes a dominant theme in Philippians. Paul sincerely believes he and fellow believers can "work out [their] own salvation" together, with the gracious energy provided by God and Christ (2:12-13 NRSV). Yet the work is not easy. The way is not smooth. The salvation marathon demands total Christ commitment: all in "in Christ" who "emptied himself" and "humbled himself... to the point of death—even death on a cross" (2:7-8). Such an awesome partnership with the crucified-risen Christ sparks not only love, joy, and gratitude but also not a little "fear and trembling" (2:12).

So what do we do today with Paul's provocative, Christ-centered philosophy of life sketched in Philippians? That's a big question best "worked out" in prayerful personal study or group study with thoughtful seekers and believers. I just offer a final word here from Philippians 2:1: "If [*ei*] there is any comfort [*paraklēsis*] in Christ." Okay, that's two emphasized words.

Comfort and Encouragement

The opening "If," with which Paul also introduces the next three associated phrases, is not as "iffy" as it sounds. Of course, there's "comfort in Christ" (along with "consolation... partnership... tender affection and sympathy," to fill out 2:1)—a lot of comfort, in fact, not just a tidbit implied by "any." Paul's rhetorical "if" clause tilts toward, "Since there is much comfort in Christ." But its conditional color still leaves the matter open in terms of response: If you acknowledge and accept there is comfort in Christ—which, of course, there is—you will experience and enjoy such comfort. But that requires engagement, active participation in Christ's story and community amid uncomfortable circumstances, as a means of pressing through hard times. Still, Pastor Paul, writing out of his own struggles in a prison cell, knows his counsel is easier said than done; he thus provides a measure of space in that little "if" word for doubt and anxiety to find their way to faith and assurance. I know I need that space.

Then there's that wonderful "comfort" (*paraklēsis*) word, which opens more interpretive space. Paul uses it several times in his writings (e.g., 2 Corinthians 1:3-7; 7:4, 7, 13; Philemon 7), though only this once in Philippians. But its spirit permeates the letter. The term has two strands of meaning, both of which apply to Philippians 2:1 and Paul's experience of life in Christ. The first strand is the "comfort" layer, as the NRSVue translates, rendered as "encouragement" in other versions (CEB, NASB, NIV). Overall, Philippians is an upbeat letter. While Paul is honest about his and the Philippians' common struggles, he doesn't whine about them or rail against them. He aims to share with his spiritual family the comfort and encouragement embodied in the sympathetic Christ.

Challenge and Urgency

The other strand of *paraklēsis* is sterner but no less significant: The emotional nurture of comfort and encouragement is entwined with the motivational spur of challenge and urgency. The verb form, *parakaleō*, literally means "call alongside," which can involve calling someone alongside to comfort and encourage them or to challenge and urge them to change some attitude or behavior. Paul calls out two church leaders: "I urge (*parakaleō*) Euodia and I urge (*parakaleō*) Syntyche to be of the same mind in the Lord" (4:2). Other versions read "I exhort" (NCB) or "I plead with" (NIV). Paul is not making a casual suggestion to these disputing women for them to take or leave; rather, he lodges an urgent plea to action for their own good and the good of the congregation.

Indeed, the entire letter of Philippians should be marked *Urgent!* for all readers, including us today. Not urgent in a panicky sense—though again, a little "fear and trembling" (2:12) can be useful to focus our attention on "what really matters" (1:10)—but in a purposeful sense of taking seriously Paul's advice about life-and-death concerns and acting upon them. We're back to the importance of engagement and active participation with God, Christ, the Holy Spirit, the apostle Paul, the Philippian believers, and "all the saints in Christ Jesus" (1:1) in living the Christ-centered life: thinking, feeling, doing, living together the life that is Christ "in any and all circumstances" (4:12), one step, stumble, and struggle at a time.

Paul unfolds his secret of life not only to enlighten our minds but to enliven our entire beings and certainly not to create some separatist secret society but to form (and keep reforming) a compassionate community of Christ-followers who "shine like stars in the world" (2:15) for the well-being of all people and creation. Paul invites us—yes, urges us—to accept the challenge of living out the life of the crucified-risen Christ in our world today.

Benediction

Paul typically ends his letters with a blessing. It's short in Philippians, but no less significant: "The grace of the Lord Jesus Christ be with your spirit" (4:23). The dominant grace note is crucial, echoing Paul's opening greeting (1:2) and embracing of the Philippian community as "partners in God's grace" (1:7). Living in Christ, running with and toward Christ, is only possible in the strength God graciously shares through Christ (we run a grace-race, remember [3:1-16]).

I supplement this pithy benediction with an old traditional blessing (and a few modern adaptations), focused on the dynamic, all-encompassing presence and partnership of Christ:

May Christ go behind you to watch your back and nudge you in the right direction.

May Christ go above you to watch over you and help you see the "big picture."

May Christ go beneath you to pick you up when you fall and carry you when needed.

May Christ go beside you, arm in arm, to comfort and encourage you and challenge and urge you on.

May Christ live in you and you in Christ to energize and equip you for a meaningful, peaceful, joyful life now and evermore. Amen.

FURTHER READING

Online Resources

I highly recommend two free, up-to-date online resources for biblical study written by ecumenical scholars for general audiences:

- Bible Odyssey (https://www.bibleodyssey.org/), written by members of the Society of Biblical Literature, the flagship organization for biblical scholars.
- Enter the Bible (https://enterthebible.org/), superintended by the stellar faculty at Luther Seminary (St. Paul, Minnesota).

Both have helpful materials for investigating Philippians. Here are my contributions to these resources:

- Spencer, F. Scott. "Famous Philippians." June 20, 2017. https://www.bibleodyssey.org/articles/famous-philippians/
- Spencer, F. Scott. "Explore the Biblical Book: Philippians." Revised from an article by Paul S. Berge. April 2023. https://enterthebible.org/book/philippians
- Spencer, F. Scott. "The Joy of Reading Paul's Letter to the Philippians." January 9, 2025. https://enterthebible.org/the-joy-of-reading-pauls-letter-to-the-philippians

Commentaries on Philippians

A wealth of fine commentaries on Philippians have been published over the past three decades. Here are six worth consulting:

Further Reading

Fee, Gordon D. *Paul's Letter to the Philippians.* The New International Commentary on the New Testament. Eerdmans, 1995.
A comprehensive academic, yet accessible, study teeming with insight from a broad evangelical perspective. A classic in the NICNT series.

Holloway, Paul A. *Philippians.* Hermeneia. Fortress Press, 2017.
A historical-critical commentary emphasizing an overarching framework of "consolation." A demanding, technical analysis, but not beyond the reach of serious nonspecialist students. Its use of Greek language in Greek font limits its accessibility, but it consistently provides English translations.

Osiek, Carolyn. *Philippians, Philemon.* Abingdon New Testament Commentaries. Abingdon Press, 2000.
A compact commentary by a leading Catholic biblical scholar with special expertise in social-historical issues. It deserves its place in this respected commentary series (ANTC), widely used by pastors, teachers, and students.

Silva, Moisés. *Philippians.* Baker Exegetical Commentary on the New Testament. Second edition. Baker Academic Press, 2005.
A careful, well-written exegetical commentary focusing on the language, grammar, style, argument, and theology of Philippians by an expert in biblical linguistic analysis.

Thompson, James W., and Bruce W. Longenecker. *Philippians and Philemon.* Paideia. Baker Academic Press, 2016.
A solid contribution to a superb Cultural, Exegetical, Historical, and Theological Bible Commentary series (Paideia). Analyses of key cultural and historical contexts of Philippians are enhanced by numerous illustrations and photographs.

Thurston, Bonnie B., and Judith Ryan. *Philippians and Philemon*. Sacra Pagina 10. Liturgical Press, 2005.
An insightful work in a major Catholic commentary series (Sacra Pagina) dedicated to making scholarly study of sacred scripture accessible to Christian ministers and laypersons.

Studies on Philippians

Fredrickson, David E. *Eros and the Christ: Longing and Envy in Paul's Christology*. Paul in Critical Contexts. Fortress Press, 2013.
A brilliant, challenging study unpacking a provocative interpretation of Christ's "self-emptying" in the Philippians Christ-hymn as an expression of passionate, melting longing to be with human beings and all creation as intimately and sympathetically as possible.

Gupta, Nijay K. "Philippians." In *The State of Pauline Studies: A Survey of Recent Research*. Edited by Nijay K. Gupta, Erin M. Heim, and Scot McKnight. Baker Academic Press, 2024.
A superb survey of the current state of scholarship on Philippians. A great place to start to get the lay of the land for an in-depth study of this letter.

Jennings, Mark A. *The Price of Partnership in the Letter of Paul to the Philippians: "Make My Joy Complete."* Library of New Testament Studies 548. Bloomsbury T&T Clark, 2018.
An informative, detailed treatment of important issues in Philippians surrounding finances, fellowship (*koinōnia*), and friendship.

Peter Oakes. *Empire, Economics, and the New Testament*. Eerdmans, 2020.
A fascinating investigation of the social, economic, and political world of the New Testament in the pervasive context of the Roman Empire. It offers much valuable material related to Philippians, especially in chapters 6, 7, and 10.

NOTES

Foreword

1 James Taylor, "The Secret O' Life," on *JT,* Columbia Records, 1977.

Chapter 2

1. Melissa Kirsch, "Social Distance," *New York Times,* March 15, 2025.
2 Sally Rooney, *Beautiful World, Where Are You* (Picador Paper, 2021), 77.
3 Aristotle. *On Rhetoric: A Theory of Civic Discourse,* trans. George A. Kennedy, 2nd ed. (Oxford University Press, 2007), 2.5.

Chapter 3

1 "Just a Formality," *Everybody Loves Raymond,* season 7, episode 15, directed by Gary Halvorson, written by Phil Rosenthal, Steve Skrovan, and Ray Romano, originally aired February 3, 2003, on CBS.
2 Aristotle, *On Rhetoric,* 2.5.
3 Aristotle, *On Rhetoric,* 2.5.
4 Mary Chapin Carpenter, "I Feel Lucky," on *Come On Come On,* Columbia Records, 1992.

Chapter 4

1 Jürgen Moltmann, *The Crucified God: The Cross of Christ as the Foundation and Criticism of Christian Theology*, trans. R. A. Wilson, John Bowden, and Margaret Kohl (Fortress Press, 1993).
2 Thomas à Kempis, *The Imitation of Christ,* trans. Leo Sherley-Price (Penguin, 1952).

Chapter 5

1 Adam Grant, *Think Again: The Power of Knowing What You Don't Know* (Viking, 2023), 1, 46–49, 52–54, 116–19.

2 Grant, *Think Again*, 70.

Chapter 6

1 Jürgen Moltmann, *The Living God and the Fullness of Life*, trans. Margaret Kohl (Westminster John Knox, 2015), 88, 90. (emphasis in original)

2 Marie Kondo, *Spark Joy: An Illustrated Master Class on the Art of Organizing and Tidying Up* (Ten Speed, 2016).

3 Taylor, "The Secret O' Life."

www.ingramcontent.com/pod-product-compliance
Lightning Source LLC
LaVergne TN
LVHW031411140826
845706LV00032B/415

* 9 7 8 1 7 9 1 0 3 6 3 6 2 *